"Even though you may have already applied to college, been accepted, and walked down the aisle to receive your high school diploma, your college prep is incomplete if you haven't prepared yourself to face and respond in a Christian way to the challenges of life on campus. *Freshman* just might be the most valuable part of your college orientation."

—WALT MUELLER, president, The Center for Parent/Youth Understanding

"The percentage of Christian students who fail to prosper in the faith after high school graduation represents a crisis. What Mark has written is truthful. It is wise. *Freshman* gives students a stretch without leaving them behind and touches the heart as well as the mind. Church leaders need to ensure that every high school graduate has a copy before taking on the college world."

—RICHARD ROSS, professor of student ministry, Southwestern Baptist Theological Seminary, Fort Worth, Texas; spokesperson, True Love Waits Campaign

"We all have heard sad stories of how our Christian students go off to college and make poor choices. *Freshman* is a resource that every senior needs to read to be prepared to stay on the path to full devotion to Christ."

—BO BOSHERS, executive director of student ministries, Willow Creek Association

"I wish my parents or youth minister had given me a resource like this before I went off to college! The chapter on how to wisely choose friends is critical as well as the discussion of relationships and sexual integrity, given the current college campus cultural climate. Every high school senior should read this book."

—JAY SEDWICK, Ph.D., associate professor of Christian Education, Dallas Theological Seminary

"This book is a great resource in preparing youth to not only enter college but also live out a journey that educates them spirit, soul, and body once on campus. Mark's exploration of godly wisdom is a must-read for Christian youth. In addition to raising the issue of real wisdom, he addresses the various barriers and challenges that young adults face in navigating life."

—EFREM SMITH, M.A., pastor, The Sanctuary Covenant Church, Minneapolis, author of *Raising Up Young Heroes*

Go Ahead:

TH1NK:

about God

about life

about others

Faith isn't just an act; it's something you live—something huge and sometimes unimaginable. By getting into the real issues in your life, TH1NK books open opportunities to talk honestly about your faith, your relationship with God and others, as well as all the things life throws at you.

Don't let other people th1nk for you . . .

TH1NK for yourself.

www.th1nkbooks.com

FRESHMAN

THE COLLEGE STUDENT'S GUIDE TO DEVELOPING WISDOM

Mark Matlock

TH1NK Books
an imprint of NavPress®

TH1NK
P.O. Box 35001
Colorado Springs, Colorado 80935

TH1NK is an imprint of NavPress.
TH1NK and the TH1NK logo are registered trademarks of NavPress. Absence of ® in connection with
marks of NavPress or other parties does not indicate an absence of registration of those marks.

ISBN 1-57683-729-7

Cover design by BURNKIT (www.burnkit.com)
Cover photograph by Photodisc
Creative Team: Gabe Filkey, Arvid Wallen, Chris Watz, Cara Iverson, Pat Miller

Matlock, Mark.
 Freshman : the college student's guide to developing wisdom / Mark
Matlock.
    p. cm.
 Includes bibliographical references (p.   ).
 ISBN 1-57683-729-7
 1. College students--Religious life. 2. Christian life. I. Title.
 BV4531.3.M38 2005
 248.8'34--dc22
                                2004027762
Printed in the United States of America

3 4 5 6 7 8 9 10 / 09 08 07 06 05

FOR A FREE CATALOG OF
NAVPRESS BOOKS & BIBLE STUDIES,
CALL 1-800-366-7788 (USA)
OR 1-800-839-4769 (CANADA)

This book is dedicated to Steve Mattson, a senior when I was a freshman, who took the time to help me find my way and died before I would become a senior myself.

CONTENTS

ACKNOWLEDGMENTS

I'd like to recognize Pat Springle, Chris Watz, and Laura Wright for their tremendous contributions to these written words. And thanks to Joel Barofsky for editing this book from a freshman's perspective.

Also, my 2004 Summer Interns—Carrie Collier, Matt Davidson, Nathan Presley, Drew Ridley, Jaclyn Summers, Jeanna Thompson, Stacy Sewell, Kim Beecham, Amber Troutman—who for several weeks of their summer joined me in ministry and allowed me to probe them for freshman experiences to apply to this book. Thank you so much.

SECTION 1

PACKING YOUR BAGS:
WISDOM GEAR FOR
THE JOURNEY

WHAT DO I NEED TO GET STARTED?

You'd think the best thing you could do as you enter college is sign up for the right classes. Or maybe buy the perfect hoodie. Select the best meal plan? If not those, it must be declaring your major. But those decisions are only peripheral to what's most important: developing wisdom. As you go about this adventure they call student life, the best decision you can make is to seek wisdom and make it the foundation of all your other decisions.

We all admire wise people, but how does one become wise? If you are a freshman, you've got a lot of concerns on your plate. Wisdom is what you need to sort them all out rather than just relying on someone else's suggestions. This book is designed to guide you through the beginning of your wisdom journey. As a freshman, you are about to enter one of the biggest transition periods in your life. You'll be reexamining who you are, what you want, what you stand for, and who you want to share your life with. If you complete this book, you will learn specific tools and skills that will accelerate your ability to understand and apply wisdom in your life.

Wisdom is a very elusive thing to discuss and apply successfully in your life. Because wisdom is more than simply learning new things, this book is divided into two sections. Section 1 seeks to explore and demystify wisdom. It uncovers why it isn't as sexy as other things in the world. I also work to define wisdom by sharing my own journey and by borrowing insight from the wisest man to ever live: Solomon. In this section, I'll share thoughts on how to stay on the right path in any situation you might face using three "points of reference." The section finishes by explaining the human limitations of wisdom and how common "speed bumps" in your life can either further your walk with God and others or lead you down a path of frustration and resentment.

Section 2 helps you apply wisdom in common crossroads of college life. In it you'll discover how and why the tools developed earlier assist you in staying aligned with God's perspective—during the breakthroughs and the swamps. Although this section can be read selectively based on whatever issue you may be facing, it's best to read it sequentially and come back to a specific chapter later as it applies to your life.

Because *Freshman* is from the TH1NK line of books, I've tried to leave room for you to do just that: think. In order to grow in wisdom, you must first deal with it intellectually, emotionally, and spiritually on your own as well as in dialogue with others. The discussion questions at the end of each chapter are intended to help you with that. Take time to work through the questions. Jot down your responses, and use a notebook if you don't have enough room in this book. A lot of people are on the same journey with similar hopes and fears, so find a few who are serious about learning to live by God's wisdom. Together you can help each other grow.

WHAT IS WISDOM?
AND WHY ISN'T IT SEXY?

His eyes hurt.

His head throbbed.

Sunlight streamed through a one-inch slit in the drapes. He turned to look at the girl next to him in the bed. He couldn't believe it—he'd done it again. He'd been partying (*one more beer couldn't hurt, could it?*), flirted with a cute girl, and ended up not only messing around with her but completing the deed as well. They did have sex, didn't they? He could hardly remember. He slid off the bed and flopped onto the carpet, then waded through clothing and puddles of reeking alcohol. The energy that had activated the frat house the night before was gone. Nobody was moving but him. His roommate slept, arm thrown over some other nameless female, drool soaking the pillow. *How did I get into this situation? What had gone so wrong in the last several months?* He threw on his clothes and bolted. *This is the way she would want it,* he told himself. *How could I stop it? She wanted it just as much as I did.*

When he arrived at his dorm, he took a shower to try to wash lingering smells from his skin, but he was really trying to cleanse the inside. Yet he couldn't feel clean because he hadn't taken the time to figure out what went so wrong. Unless he searched deep inside himself for the answer, the cycle was likely to repeat itself.

"I THINK I'LL MESS UP MY LIFE TODAY"

Very few of us wake up with the goal of messing up our lives. In fact, one of the driving forces for attending college is the desire to make the most of our lives. But poor decisions—even the small ones—can ultimately devastate us and those around us. As a minister, I have the privilege of walking with people through some of the greatest joys and deepest pains of their lives. In just the past few days, I've talked to an unmarried college girl who found out she's pregnant. She isn't even sure who the father is. I've talked to another student whose parents' unresolved bitterness has finally led them to divorce. The whole family is deeply depressed and furious, leaving the student frustrated and wanting to vent in some way but not sure the right way to vent.

None of these people intended to be in those situations. They didn't wake up one morning and say, "I think I'll completely ruin my life today by making a stupid decision." No, they made foolish little decisions that led to others, and still others, until one day they found their lives speeding in the wrong direction. The result feels like a war zone, lives pockmarked by the bullet holes and shattered by the explosions of destructive decisions.

No, not everyone is on the brink of destruction. And even if you do make a string of bad decisions, it's not a guarantee that you'll completely destroy your life. But the list of college pressures and excitements can really stress a person out. You might be worrying about which college major is best for you or wondering if you should change roommates because yours is driving you crazy. Or maybe you're hoping you'll find the right friends or even "the one." Situations like these make it even more obvious that if you want to make the most of your college years, you'll need wisdom.

The good news is that no matter where you are in life, wisdom is not far away.

You already know that going to college opens the door to a new world of possibilities. If you live in a dorm or your own apartment, the first couple of weeks are like summer camp. Your parents aren't around, and there are no curfews. Nobody is looking over your shoulder, so you can do whatever you want. You make new friends. There are parties almost every night. Students egg each other on to do something a little crazier, a little wilder, sometimes a little more dangerous. Things start out pretty tame, but before you know it, you may find yourself in situations you hadn't planned—situations that have the potential to be really destructive.

Instead of letting bad things happen, you can use wisdom to help you develop a pattern of life that takes advantage of the new freedoms (you can still have fun) but doesn't hurt you, your college life, or anything else important to you. That's part of developing wisdom. Plus I'm going to share some wisdom I've gained on my journey so far—why wisdom's often overlooked, what it is exactly, what can stop its progress in your life, and how to apply it to some specific college situations. In doing so, my goal is to help you make the most of your college experience. I want to help you have a great time while learning to avoid some of life's pitfalls.

17

FREEDOM AND THE PRODIGAL SON

Most people would agree that it's instructive to learn valuable lessons from punishment and painful consequences for poor choices. But most would also agree that it would be far better to not make those choices in the first place. In the story of the prodigal son, Jesus tells about a young man who decides to go off on his own. He takes some of his dad's cash and heads off. Never having had financial freedom before, he blows his money and does nothing to multiply the opportunities presented by his upbringing and surroundings. And then what happens? He ends up on his knees, eating pig food and begging his father to take him back (see Luke 15:11-21).

If only the prodigal son would have considered the consequences of what he was about to do before he did it. See, wisdom is taking our knowledge of the way God works and applying it to our world. No, we cannot know God's mind perfectly, but He has revealed His take on life in nature and in His Word. It is one thing to know the best choice, but wisdom is the tool we'll need to actually act on it.

After reaping the consequences of his rash actions, the prodigal son musters up the courage to act, and the result is still favorable. He chose to learn from his mistakes by swallowing his pride, and in doing so, he took a key step in the right direction. He stepped toward wisdom, not away from it.

DEFINING WISDOM

Wisdom may seem elusive and difficult to define, yet we can recognize and admire wise people when we see them. But what exactly is *wisdom*? This is a question I've been interested in for much of my life, and my definition has evolved over time. In my search, I've seen that wisdom is "the human capacity to understand life from God's perspective." Now, that is a fairly short definition, but it's got great implications. I've tinkered with this definition over time. I used to define it simply as "seeing life from God's perspective for the purpose of living well," but living for Christ is not always easy, and I wasn't certain "living well" was really the ultimate accomplishment wisdom offered.

There was also the issue of God's great knowledge and under-standing: Could I really have God's entire perspective? So I added that wisdom is the "human capacity" to understand this point of view. I also realized that because we have God's Word, it is possible to have God's perspective on life and still fail to live by it. Having wisdom does not ensure that I will follow it.

SOLOMON'S REQUEST AS THE KEY FOR DEFINING WISDOM

In the first book of Kings, God comes to Solomon offering him anything he desires. God is not in the practice of acting like a genie and granting three wishes, but in this instance, He gave Solomon an opportunity to ask Him for anything his heart desired. Realizing that he was young and fairly inexperienced at life, Solomon asked for wisdom. Why? Let's look at the biblical account for insight.

> *"Now, O LORD my God, you have made your servant king in place of my father David. But I am only a little child and do not know how to carry out my duties. Your servant is here among the people you have chosen, a great people, too numerous to count or number. So give your servant a discerning heart to govern your people and to distinguish between right and wrong. For who is able to govern this great people of yours?"*
>
> *The Lord was pleased that Solomon had asked for this. So God said to him, "Since you have asked for this and not for long life or wealth for yourself, nor have asked for the death of your enemies but for discernment in administering justice, I will do what you have asked. I will give you a wise and discerning heart, so that there will never have been anyone like you, nor will there ever be." (1 Kings 3:7-12)*

God was thrilled with Solomon's choice. Rather than asking for money, fame, power, or the perfect marriage partner, Solomon asked for a foundational skill for living successfully—wisdom—and God delighted in granting it (see James 1:5).

Realizing that he was being called to govern the people of Israel, Solomon wanted God's insight and perspective so he could do his job successfully. Essentially Solomon was asking for the ability to see life from God's perspective. Of course, we can't fully comprehend all that is in the mind of the eternal, omnipotent, all-knowing Creator of the universe, but God has given us principles and truths to trust on this side of eternity. He has wired the world to work in a certain way, and we'll benefit tremendously if we understand His ways sooner rather than later.

WISDOM IS MORE THAN GOOD CHOICES — IT'S ALSO AN ATTITUDE

Good choices are a benefit to living wisely, but the ability to make good decisions is not the end of wisdom. A wise person also has the right attitude in life and knows how to respond to others in a mature way. They, like Solomon, see the fear of the Lord as the beginning of wisdom (see Proverbs 9:10).

I like playing games, but my wife says I'm a terrible winner. Once when we played Monopoly, I made a series of good purchases and really totaled my wife in the game. During the game and afterward, I just couldn't help but gloat at my perfect execution during the game. My wife was not amused. Yes, I had won, but continually rubbing her nose in my victory was not the best response I could have had. My choices were good, but my attitude was not. Wisdom is not just about playing a perfect game, but it is also "how" you play the game.

CHAPTER 1

TWO INVITATIONS

The book of Proverbs was written by Solomon (the king of Israel and the wisest man on earth), and it's almost entirely about wisdom.

Solomon personifies wisdom and foolishness as two women, Lady Wisdom and Madame Folly, calling out to people in the city. Both women invite people to come to them, both make promises, and both give predictable results. Every day you're in college, your primary freedom is to accept one of these two invitations.

In Proverbs, Lady Wisdom invites to her home those who will listen to her when she says, "Leave your simple ways and you will live; walk in the way of understanding" (Proverbs 9:6). The promise that those who respond to her "will live" doesn't just mean they'll breathe, eat, and sleep. It means they'll *really live*. This promise reminds me of Jesus' statement, "I have come that they may have life, and have it to the full" (John 10:10) — that is, bursting with meaning, richness, and mystery. So, what does this kind of life look like? Previous chapters in Proverbs tell us that those who seek God's wisdom will be protected from the devastating consequences of foolishness and that they'll experience the positive results of physical health, peace, and strong, honest, intimate relationships. That's wisdom's promise to you and to me.

21

Meanwhile, Madame Folly is across the street, standing at the door of her house and calling to those who are walking by. Her invitation sounds exactly like the wise woman's, yet she represents foolishness. Where Lady Wisdom wants to do what is right to preserve a long and God-honoring life, Madame Folly wants to do what is exciting, what feels best, and what gives her maximum temporal pleasure. When she calls out, she's just as welcoming as Lady Wisdom, but her promise is much different. She entices people with sensual pleasure and the tempting element of danger: "Stolen water is sweet; food eaten in secret is delicious!" (Proverbs 9:17).

Madame Folly's invitation is described further in chapter 7. With seductive language, she tempts those who will listen. After she grabs a man and kisses him, she tells him that he alone is the object of her affection: "I've been looking for you—just for you" (see Proverbs 7:15). (Of course, she says this to anybody who responds to her, not just this guy.) She tells him how she has prepared her bed with the finest spices and promises that because her husband is far away they won't get caught. "Come," she purrs, "let's drink deep of love till morning; let's enjoy ourselves with love!" (Proverbs 7:18).

But instead of life, the result of responding to her temptation is death. Solomon describes the results in both chapters. First: "All at once he followed her like an ox going to the slaughter, like a deer stepping into a noose . . . little knowing it will cost him his life" (Proverbs 7:22-23). Solomon then puts a knife in the heart with this conclusion: "But little do they know that the dead are there, that her guests are in the depths of the grave" (Proverbs 9:18).

It is true that her words are filled with excitement and adventure. They make our hearts pound; we feel alive. Yet this feeling is short-lived. In the end, Madame Folly offers more than she can give. Instead of life to the fullest, we are left with only a hangover from the fleeting burst of gratification.

Folly keeps her door closed so those on the street can't see what's inside. That description reminds me of adult video stores I drive by every day. Have you ever seen one with windows? Not having windows hides the shame and embarrassment that comes from participating in foolish activities. Also, these porn shops instinctively conceal what's inside from those on the streets because it makes the shop more alluring. Inside they hide a lingering emotional and spiritual death.

Oh, come on, you might be thinking. *My decisions aren't life-or-death choices.* True, your daily choices may or may not end or continue your life as you know it, but they certainly determine the *quality* of your life. Each foolish choice you make can eventually rob you of meaning, hope, and joy and take you a step toward shame, discouragement, and loneliness.

Whose invitation will you choose today? You need to choose intentionally, because whether you're aware of it or not, you choose without thought all the time, every day.

WHAT'S WRONG WITH WISDOM?

If wisdom is so terrific, why isn't it the hottest topic around? There's a simple answer to that question: it's because in our culture, the call of foolishness is depicted as incredibly attractive, sensuous, a bit dangerous, and often without major consequences. In our movies, unfaithfulness is often viewed as true romance, as life lived to the fullest. Sure, there will be some consequences, but they are worth it, for what we did made us feel liberated, intoxicated, and "drunk with love." Take for instance four Academy Award-winners for "Best Picture" from 1996 to 1999. All of the films—*American Beauty, Shakespeare in Love, Titanic,* and *The English Patient*—involved relationships in which cheating was a source of great enjoyment and passion.

In *The Tipping Point,*[1] Malcolm Gladwell proposes the real reason people smoke. In an effort to reduce smoking, large campaigns were started to inform people of the risks and hazards of smoking cigarettes. His informal research revealed that most people who smoked "overstated" the risks of smoking, believing it was actually worse than science revealed. The information had not made a difference; in fact, people thought the consequences of their actions would be much worse. The reason most people smoked cigarettes, Gladwell's research indicated, was because of a fond memory they had of someone "cool" who smoked. More than any other vice out there, I have always been intrigued with smoking. The reason? I had a cool babysitter who would secretly smoke when she took care of me, and I connected with her rebellion. Wisdom often works the same way. We "know" what is best for us, but it's not usually what's most intriguing to us.

Our perception of wisdom is completely and tragically messed up. For some reason, we think it's not as marketable as sexual unfaithfulness or getting into dangerous fights, as the movies would suggest. Many people have told me they value the *concept* of wisdom and realize it offers some inherent benefits to their lives and relationships, but they rarely accept wisdom's invitation. Why not? When Madame Folly says that "stolen water is sweet" and "food eaten in secret is delicious," she is referring to the "buzz" that comes from doing the wrong thing.

Our view of wisdom probably is that it's not that sexy, but what is our concept of a fulfilling, fun life? Solomon says we should look for wisdom "as for silver and search for it as for hidden treasure" (Proverbs 2:4) because he knows that's where the real fulfillment comes from, regardless of its lack of surface "sex appeal."

In order to search for wisdom, we first must realize that all that glitters isn't gold and that wisdom is a treasure of tremendous value that doesn't always glitter. We must search, struggle, and sacrifice to see beyond the surface and realize that wisdom is a treasure we simply must have, like diamonds in their original state of carbon.

WISDOM AS A JOURNEY

Developing wisdom is a journey, and none of us arrives at the destination on this side of eternity. When I think of this journey, I think of two of my favorite epic movies, *Star Wars* and *The Lord of the Rings*. I was young when *Star Wars* came out. At that time, Darth Vader was just a villain, but as the movies continued to develop, we realized that he is really the main character. After George Lucas released episodes one through three (which were released a couple decades *after* episodes four through six), we saw that Darth Vader began as the young and innocent Anakin Skywalker. As he enters the adolescent stage of life, he starts to experiment with a rebellious and reckless spirit, rejecting the wisdom and counsel of others. As he goes into the adult phase of life, he chooses the allure of the world's wisdom and eventually goes astray.

25

In *The Lord of the Rings*, Frodo undergoes quite a journey too, but with different results. Growing up in the shire, Frodo lives a simple life in which he is rarely tempted or challenged. As his time of maturity comes, he is given a huge responsibility to bear—the ring of Sauron—requiring him to leave the comfort and safety of home. When he steps away from the safe "bubble" of the shire, he encounters ferocious battles and temptations that nearly consume him. However, unlike Anakin, he chooses to align himself with the wise council of those who are more concerned with truth than with selfish gain. Sure, he encounters pitfalls along the way, but with the help of Gandalf (mentor), Sam (friend), and others, he always manages to find his way back to the right path. Your life may not always be as cinematic as the characters on the silver screen, but each of us is on the beginning of a journey, a quest all our own. Wisdom can make the difference.

THINK ABOUT IT

1. As you look at the college experience, which aspects of it excite you? Which parts scare you? Explain.

2. How different might the prodigal son's life have been if he had stepped toward wisdom before demanding his inheritance from his father?

3. Do you agree with the author's definition of wisdom as "the human capacity to understand life from God's perspective"? Why or why not?

4. Read Proverbs 7–9. What do you think about having two invitations in college, one by Lady Wisdom and the other by Madame Folly? In what specific areas do these invitations surface in your life? Whose invitation do you usually take?

27

5. What are some reasons the woman of foolishness is attractive to so many people? (What does she offer that people want?) Why do so many people think wisdom is not as attractive as foolishness?

6. How do you think the metaphor of a journey fits with the pursuit of wisdom?

7. What are some things you hope to gain from reading this book?

POINTS OF REFERENCE:
WHERE AM I ON
MY WISDOM JOURNEY?

It seems to me that wisdom comes in two flavors. In the book of James, a distinction is made between wisdom from the world and wisdom from heaven:

> *Who is wise and understanding among you? Let him show it by his good life, by deeds done in the humility that comes from wisdom. But if you harbor bitter envy and selfish ambition in your hearts, do not boast about it or deny the truth. Such "wisdom" does not come down from heaven but is earthly, unspiritual, of the devil. For where you have envy and selfish ambition, there you find disorder and every evil practice.*
>
> *But the wisdom that comes from heaven is first of all pure; then peace-loving, considerate, submissive, full of mercy and good fruit, impartial and sincere. Peacemakers who sow in peace raise a harvest of righteousness.*
> *(James 3:13-18)*

Our understanding of wisdom is incomplete if we do not understand the concept of alignment. In describing the two "types" of wisdom, we quickly see that heavenly wisdom is aligned with the things of God, and worldly wisdom is aligned with our selfish ambitions and the Devil.

ALIGNMENT

In Proverbs 22:1, we learn that a good name is more valuable than gold. Now, there are people who would tell you that getting ahead financially—whatever the moral cost—is more important than a good reputation. That is worldly wisdom. How many times have you heard a celebrity say, "I don't care what other people think," to justify their actions after they have done something shameful or embarrassing? But God tells us there are many things more valuable than riches: a good reputation, wisdom, and a devoted spouse.

If I align my thinking with worldly wisdom, my source will be fallible; I might say, "I think this is right" or "My friends value this," but people are weak standards. However, if I align my life with heavenly wisdom, I look to God and His Word as my standards. Without a proper posture (of humility and awe) toward God, we will never adopt His ways. Without proper alignment, we cannot grow in "heavenly wisdom."

Solomon enjoyed many wonderful experiences in his life as he applied and executed wisdom. He ruled during the most peaceful and prosperous time in Israel's history. But Solomon later made some serious mistakes that caused him great pain. His wisdom was thrown out of alignment. First he married wives who worshiped other gods, and then he listened to them rather than being obedient to the Lord (see 1 Kings 11:1-8). Even armed with this great ability, wisdom has to be put into action for it to be effective. With this insight, I learned that wisdom is something we can possess but not something that always guarantees making perfect choices.

TRIANGULATING WISDOM'S POINTS OF REFERENCE

It's time to pack our bags with the basic gear we'll need on our journey to developing wisdom. During college, I took a survival class in which we learned to, well, survive. Because the final for the class involved our being left alone in the woods to use our skills, this was a class I paid serious attention in. I could not fail the final.

Being left alone in the woods without any reference point for finding the way back can be frightening. You could find your way around if you possessed and understood how to use a compass and a map of the area. In our hi-tech world, you might use a GPS system to find your way (as long as the batteries were charged). This device uses "triangulation" to determine your location. By using three satellites as reference points, the receiver can help you understand exactly where you are within a matter of feet. Armed with a GPS and a map of the area, you would be able to align yourself on the right path and remain on it as long as you had access to the satellites' positions in the sky.

Similarly, the beginning of wisdom occurs when you are properly aligned with God's perspective. The next several chapters will help you understand the three "points of reference" you will use to identify where you are on your wisdom journey. The definition I offer—wisdom is "the human capacity to understand life from God's perspective"—puts the concept simply but does not give you any handles for actually developing wisdom in your life. I'm going to do the best I can to do that for you.

Along my wisdom journey, I read numerous commentaries on Proverbs. In the commentaries, the proverbs were organized by groups of twenty-one, ten, and seven. Because none of the breakdowns seemed quite refined or complete, I wrote every proverb on a 3x5 card and divided the cards into piles on the floor. I kept at this until I could put almost any proverb in at least one pile. I dubbed the three piles "cause-and-effect relationships," "values," and "justice"—the three points of reference aligning ourselves with God's wisdom.

I eventually realized that if I could observe life through these three filters, I would be learning the essence of wisdom each day while growing in wisdom in my own life. All three "points of alignment" are present in every situation we are in. Let's look at each point briefly before unpacking them more deeply in the next chapters.

Cause-and-effect relationships are essential in helping us discern the impact of choices we make in life. Having an understanding of how certain events are related is a skill the wise have mastered.

32

Values reveal what we believe has worth and is desirable. So many decisions that must be made in life are affected by how much or little we value a person, object, life, or concept. Possessing the right values is critical to our pursuit of wisdom. Because we are infected with sin and are often influenced by a godless society, God becomes our source of learning what to value. And in addition to God, we can often learn through life's experiences about what is valuable.

Justice gives us our understanding of right and wrong. We tend to think of justice in terms of punishment, but it also involves knowing how to reward. A wise person treats others with fairness, is truthful in his or her dealings, and shows God's grace to others.

JESUS AS WISDOM LIVED OUT PERFECTLY

Nobody has ever been more aligned with God, and therefore more wise, than Jesus (no, not even Solomon). How do we know how great God is? By looking at Christ. He was "the Word made flesh" (see John 1:14). His life personified skillful living. He valued the right things, and He patterned His life after His Father's will. He was totally and completely absorbed in doing whatever the Father wanted Him to do by "perfectly" living out both the Great Commandment and the Great Commission. He loved God with all His heart, soul, mind, and strength; He loved His neighbor as Himself and showed His purpose was to "seek and to save what was lost" (Luke 19:10) by "making all things new" (see 2 Corinthians 5:17) through His death on the cross. His message to you and me is to follow His example.

As we follow Jesus, our lives will become anything but boring. They will be rich and meaningful.

A MISCONCEPTION ABOUT WISDOM

Like the plot of a great movie, pursuing Christ and His wisdom leads us through times of certainty and times of mystery. Over time, some things will become crystal clear, but God's path for each of us takes us through twists and turns in our life's story. At times, we will see as clearly as a climber standing atop a mountain on a sunny summer day, and other times, we'll be in the foggy valleys, groping to find the trail. Even those who were around Jesus and heard Him teach "groped in the darkness" (see Acts 13:11). His parables and teachings were difficult, and often the disciples asked Him to explain what He was talking about. Both certainty and mystery are important parts of the path to gaining God's wisdom, and wisdom demands that we embrace both so we can grow.

But growing in wisdom does not mean we will see exactly as God does. In his classic book *Knowing God*,[2] J. I. Packer said that many people have a misunderstanding about God's wisdom. They believe a truly wise person is so in touch with God that he knows exactly what God is doing all the time, much like an air traffic controller keeps track of all the planes on his screen. Instead, wisdom is like the headlights of a car at night. With God's wisdom, we see just enough ahead to keep us on the right path—no more, no less.

Seeing the world from God's perspective is not like having a crystal ball. While God's wisdom is constantly guiding us into truth and light, our human condition often puts us into shadow and fog. Often our limited ability to see God's perspective fully makes trusting in wisdom difficult and trying. We'll look at those times later in the book, but for now, realize that the will and ways of God are not simple and easy. If Jesus experienced dark, difficult, and painful moments, can we expect much less? If we believe God's wisdom is a crystal ball that always shows us what to do, we'll be deeply disappointed. But if we realize that God's will is right even when it is difficult, we'll be willing to sacrifice our pride by "[fixing] our eyes on Jesus, the author and perfecter" (Hebrews 12:2)—the One who "learned obedience [alignment] from what he suffered" (Hebrews 5:8).

In the next chapters, we'll start learning more about each point of reference, how each is useful in developing wisdom, and what can get you lost in your pursuit of wisdom.

CHAPTER 2

THINK ABOUT IT

1. What does Solomon's life (his successes and failures) teach us about wisdom? Commit to doing a biblical study of Solomon's life for more background (see 1 Kings, 2 Chronicles, Proverbs, Ecclesiastes, Song of Solomon).

2. Do you agree that there are two types of wisdom, as illustrated by James? Examine each element of James 3:13-18 carefully. How does each characteristic of the world's wisdom and God's wisdom play out in your life?

3. What is the connection between Jesus and the pursuit of wisdom?

4. The benefits of wisdom are protection, confidence, and a good reputation. Which of these is most attractive to you at this point? Explain.

DISCERNING THE DEEP:
UNDERSTANDING CAUSE AND EFFECT

We learn in science class that for every action there is an equal and opposite reaction. Life is made up of similar situations. While they may not be hard-and-fast laws, actions produce consequences that can be either negative or positive. The wise person is able to forecast a probable portrait of the future based on certain actions and their most likely reactions. The wise person can also find deeper meaning when seeing only surface indications because he understands the relationships of these things.

I'm a big fan of the television program *CSI*. I know it isn't terribly realistic (science can't always get the bad guys), but it is fun to watch. I like the way a coroner is able to examine certain wounds on the hands or discolorations on the neck to be able to determine what the cause of death might have been. These surface indicators, combined with an understanding of the relationship of cause and effect, give great insight that to the untrained eye would be invisible or ignored.

The ability to effectively discern how things are impacting us and how we are impacting others relies heavily on our ability to understand the relationships that exist between causes and effects. There are certain activities that God says will improve our lives and others that He declares will cause us to lose joy. The world chases many different goals than we do, and so this point of reference is important if we are to remain in alignment with God's perspective.

DISCERNING ISSUES – BIG OR SMALL?

Some of you are beginning to think this chapter is going to be predictable. *I know where this is going*, you think. *He's going to talk about obvious, trite, cliché examples regarding all the bad choices I could make and their consequences: if I do drugs, I will fry my brain; if I cut classes, my grades will drop; if I have sex, I will expose myself to sexually transmitted diseases and might even cause a pregnancy. Cause and effect*, you say to yourself, *I've heard this before.*

Most of us have been sufficiently warned about the consequences of some of the "big" issues of life. What I love about this reference point is that we see the subtlety of a wise life. It is rarely in the big issues of life that a person becomes wise; it's in the way one handles the hundreds and thousands of smaller details of life. Here are three subtle examples of cause-and-effect relationships that we can learn from Proverbs. They require discerning deeper, more hidden areas of life rather than the blatant big issues we usually hear about in youth group or Sunday morning services.

38

If a man loudly blesses his neighbor early in the morning, it will be taken as a curse. (Proverbs 27:14)

There was a really sweet girl I knew in college, and in all the years I have known her, I can think of only a couple of times she's been grumpy. She has a "when life gives you lemons, make lemonade" kind of attitude. I'm happy for her. Just to preface what I'm about to say, I am not a morning person. In fact, I hate mornings and therefore planned most of my class schedule to avoid mornings. But every now and then, I'd be in some situation where I would *have* to wake up early. So here my friend Miss Sunny-Sunshine comes, bopping along over to my table to greet me. "Happy, happy, joy, joy" was not the mood I was in, and even though she meant no harm, her blissful cheeriness was making me furious. A wise person knows how and when to approach a person.

And then there's my friend, let's call him Brian, who lived in my residence hall. As soon as I came out of my dorm room, he would get in my face regardless of my mood and start talking to me. Nice guy, but I actually started doing everything in my power to avoid him because it was just too much. There's a proverb that speaks to this: "Be careful of knocking on your neighbor's door or he may become sick of you" (see Proverbs 25:17).

That's a really strange thing for God to include in His Word, don't you think? Of all the important things, why that? Because it is important. God uses us to bring His message of good news to others, but if we drive everyone around us nuts, it doesn't matter how great a message it is we bear. No one will listen. Being successful in the small things in life provides a solid platform for the more important issues.

39

Yanking a dog's ears is as foolish as interfering in someone else's argument. (Proverbs 26:17, NLT)

We had these two huge Great Danes living next to us that scared me with their wild barking every time I would near the fence. Grabbing their ears and yanking them is one of the more unpleasant things I could do. Some people always like to get involved in other people's problems. This proverb doesn't mean that we shouldn't get involved; it just warns us to be prepared for the likely result. Sometimes trying to "be the peacemaker" can really be an extension of our own pride to be spiritually successful. The wise person discerns when to be of help by getting involved and when to help by getting out of the way.

As a dog returns to its vomit, so a fool repeats his folly. (Proverbs 26:11)

Every time I do a project on wisdom, I try to get this proverb in. It is so illustrative and true. This proverb helps us see the relationship between a fool and his probability of repeating the same mistake twice (or even more often). There was a guy on our campus who was a real womanizer. He had cheated on several girlfriends and began new relationships with those he had been cheating with. Soon he was cheating on the new girls with someone else. I'll never forget a conversation I overheard as he was trying to lure another girl into a relationship. She said, "How will I know you won't cheat on me like you did those other girls?" He responded, "Baby, you're different than them. I would never do that to you." She wisely retorted, "I may be different, but you are the same fool. And I'm not letting you drag me back to your same old pool of vomit."

THE EASY WAY AND THE HARD WAY

There are two basic ways to learn wisdom: the easy way and the hard way. The easy way is to watch people and observe the effects of their choices. You can avoid a truckload of mistakes by hanging out with someone who has already made the mistakes you want to avoid (and has learned from them). My brother Jonathan is a few years younger than me. He's a terrific brother, and I think he's really wise. One day I said to him, "I'm really impressed with all you know and how you respond to situations. How did you learn to be such a wise person?"

Without a second's hesitation, he responded, "I watched you, Josh, and Jeremy, and I decided I wouldn't do the dumb things you guys have done."

Unfortunately, most of us aren't that sharp. We've had to learn things the hard way: by making our own mistakes. Pain is an excellent teacher. It's too bad so many of us sign up for that course. Wisdom is often associated with old age because the longer you've lived, the more you've observed and the more time you've had to recognize and learn from your mistakes.

But we can also learn from successes. Good decisions, like bad ones, seem to multiply themselves. When we make good choices about time, relationships, studies, or any other area of our lives, the positive effects reinforce our desire to make more wise decisions. And as we watch others succeed in these areas, we are motivated to follow their lead and make the same kind of decisions they've made. That's why reading autobiographies and biographies can be so rewarding—we can learn from others' mistakes and successes.

TAKING TIME TO DISCERN THE DEEP

We won't learn much from our surroundings unless we carve out time to reflect. College is an incredibly busy time, and we often go a hundred miles per hour from the moment we wake up till the time we go to sleep. One of the most important principles I've learned is the absolute necessity of finding regular time to think about what happened each day. Some of us can't do that in our dorm room or apartment because there's always something going on, people stopping by, and music blaring. We have to get away and find a quiet place to reflect. From my first weeks at Biola as a freshman, I became known as "The Vampire" because I walked around campus late at night when everybody else was asleep. The only people I saw were campus security. This was the time I set aside to process all I had done and seen that day. I don't know what my life would have been like without that time, but I can assure you that those walks gave me far more insight about me, my friends, God, and God's purposes for my life than anything else in my day did. Sure, all the other experiences and interactions were important, but those walks enabled me to process things so I understood them more clearly and more deeply.

I don't know what kind of time will help you process your day most effectively, but figure it out and do it. Maybe it's early in the morning (I understand that some people actually prefer early morning), or maybe it's at the library between classes. It doesn't matter when, where, or how. It only matters that you take regular time to consider the events of the day so you can observe the causes and effects. It helped me to experiment with what method worked best. Not everyone reflects in the same way. I had to play with different techniques (prayer walks or runs, journaling, hiking, getting out into nature) before becoming "The Vampire."

Taking time to reflect helps us better understand ourselves, better relate to God, and better connect with those around us going through similar emotional, spiritual, and intellectual transitions freshmen face.

GOD'S PURPOSEFUL INTENTIONS

As we step back and observe the relationship between action and reaction, cause and effect, one of the lessons we learn is that God has orchestrated the world with good, purposeful intentions. The patterns of nature and relationships are incredibly creative and beautiful. Amazingly, God even uses the darkest colors in our lives to create something wonderful in us. He did with Jesus by using one of the most horrendous methods of execution to create the opportunity for a relationship with Him. If we stop long enough to reflect and look into the past and then toward the future, the vast majority of events in our lives begin to make sense. If they don't, we need to look more closely to see a deeper, previously hidden cause and effect. That doesn't mean that everything God intends is easy and fun. No, as a loving Father, He knows we need struggle to help us grow. As we'll see later, difficulties can be a roadblock or a bridge, depending on our perceptions and responses.

Although making big decisions such as which major to choose and who to marry may not be easy, even for the wise (observe Solomon for discernment in selecting good wives), the older we get, the more often we see God's guiding hand redeeming and guiding our lives.

THINK ABOUT IT

1. Describe what life would be like if causes and effects weren't predictable.

2. Read Galatians 6:7. What is meant by "God cannot be mocked"? Why is that important in your understanding of cause and effect (sowing and reaping)?

3. Describe the short-term and long-term repercussions of not
   using wisdom with the following aspects of your life:

	SHORT-TERM	LONG-TERM
free time		
study habits		
parties		
sex		
friends		
sleeping and eating		
time to reflect		

44

4. Do you tend to learn the easy way or the hard way? Explain your answer.

5. When and how will you carve out time to reflect each day? What will be some benefits to you?

45

6. How can a person identify his stage (child, adolescent, or adult) of internalizing the principles of cause and effect? Which one best represents your life right now?

7. If you're at the child or adolescent stage, what do you need to do to move to the next stage?

CHOOSING THE RIGHT PATH:
WHY JUSTICE IS ESSENTIAL TO WISDOM

Evil men do not understand justice,
   but those who seek the LORD understand it fully.
   (Proverbs 28:5)

God made us with an innate desire for justice. We long for right to be blessed and wrong to be punished. When that doesn't happen, we feel violated. In 1994, O. J. Simpson tried to flee in his white Ford Bronco from a fleet of police cruisers on Los Angeles freeways. After his arrest, the highly publicized trial was tracked every night on network news and in detail on cable. Finally, the jury's verdict was in and O. J. was acquitted—he walked free. But a few months later, a civil trial found Simpson guilty. People across the country inherently knew a man could not be both innocent and guilty of the same crime. Justice, it seemed, was lost.

An understanding of justice is a critical reference point for our journey. In fact, it's one of the central characteristics of God Himself. When envisioning a judge, many of us think of someone wise who is able to see through conflicting information to the heart of a matter and then make an accurate, fair decision. That's what God is like. He is omniscient, knowing every detail of every person and situation. If He knows the number of hairs on our head (see Luke 12:7), He obviously isn't lacking for information. Along with knowledge, He is completely and totally just, punishing the wicked and rewarding those who do what is right.

Cause and effect shows the relationships between actions and their results. Justice is the praise or condemnation imposed on us by authority as well as the ability to discern between right and wrong. It allows us to be fair to others and take a stand against injustice in our world. (Interestingly, Jesus spoke about the injustice of not helping the poor, the widow, the oppressed, and the "least of these" more than about abortion and homosexuality.)

Many Scriptures describe God's justice. In Romans, Paul wrote about God's righteous judgment of believers who act in ways that please God and unbelievers who live for themselves:

48

> God "will give to each person according to what he has done." To those who by persistence in doing good seek glory, honor and immortality, he will give eternal life. But for those who are self-seeking and who reject the truth and follow evil, there will be wrath and anger. (Romans 2:6-8)

To some extent, we all experience God's grace. Proverbs says that God allows the rain to fall on both the wicked and the good (see Matthew 5:45). This is often referred to as "general" grace. Because of God's presence and the reality that we were made in His image, we experience many of the benefits of God even while we are in sin. In the first two chapters of Romans, we see God's depiction of wrath not so much as a specific action as much as it is a "removing" of this general grace, leaving us to our devices.

Notice that judgment is personal. God's judgment isn't

philosophical or metaphorical; it is not arbitrary. Following God pleases Him, but rejecting the One who gave His Son for us makes Him angry.

Most of us think of justice as a negative, harsh, punitive thing, but I prefer to think of it as neutral. The determination of the judge depends on the choices and actions of the one being judged. It's like those who judge figure skating or diving competitions. Those judges aren't trying to punish anyone. In fact, their desire is for participants to do their best and be rewarded. That's the perspective of most professors in college, resident assistants in the dorms, policemen, parents—and God. They don't delight in punishment (see Ezekiel 18:23). They delight in rewarding excellence and good behavior, but to be just, they hold people accountable for bad choices. The loss of rewards is enough in most cases. In his first letter to the Corinthians, Paul explained that all believers will one day stand before Christ to give an account of our actions (see 2 Corinthians 5:10). This isn't the Great White Throne judgment of unbelievers. This is the Judgment Seat of Christ, when everything we've done as Christians will pass through the testing fire of Christ. Everything we've done for His honor will result in rewards, and those things we did for impure, selfish reasons will burn up. The guilt and shame will be washed away by Christ's forgiveness, but so will the opportunity to be rewarded for doing the right thing for the right reasons.

THE PRACTICE OF JUSTICE

"Okay, Mark," you might respond to what I've said about justice so far, "but how does God's justice relate to me? I know I'll experience it someday, but does it make any difference to me now?"

As I grew in my understanding of this reference point of wisdom, I realized that justice is a reflection of God's character in us. While it is not our place to judge the wicked, it is crucial to know how to discern right from wrong, how to trust others, and how to be fair. Let's look at various proverbs that give a portrait of what justice looks like when practiced in our lives. These principles will find their way into many of life's situations.

REALIZE THERE IS AN ULTIMATE JUDGE, AND IT'S NOT US

Scripture states that the beginning of wisdom comes when we fear the Lord (see Proverbs 9:10). This fear is not simply respect; this fear is a comprehension of God's ultimate authority and our need to daily confess our arrogance and seek to love Him and others humbly. Why would we adopt His Word and values if He were not the ultimate standard who always views things correctly? In the same way, unless we understand that He is the ultimate judge, it is difficult to develop a wise sense of justice in our lives. One of the characteristics of fools in our modern society is that they have made their own ideas of right and wrong the basis for their judgments. These, however, are weak at best when viewed in contrast to the justice of God Almighty.

All a man's ways seem innocent to him, but motives are weighed by the Lord. (Proverbs 16:2)

It is significant to note that we rarely stop and reflect on the rightness or wrongness of our actions. We tend to believe that our way is right. Often our motives are difficult to discern, but the Lord is capable of judging them even when we're not. Proverbs 20:5 states, "The purposes of a man's heart are deep waters, but a man of understanding draws them out." As we grow in wisdom, we will have better insight into what really motivates a person. The psalmist writes in Psalm 139:23-24, "Search me, O God, and know my heart. . . . See if there is any offensive [hurtful] way in me, and lead me in the way everlasting." Motives are important to God in making just decisions, and when we ask God to detect our own motives, we find ourselves taking more steps to becoming wise.

Be sure of this: The wicked will not go unpunished, but those who are righteous will go free. (Proverbs 11:21)

This is an important principle in our understanding of justice. Some of us believe that if we obey God, we will continually have a good life. While this is generally true, we often get stumped when we seem to be doing all the right things and feel miserable, while our friends (or worse our enemies) go against God and seem to be living easy. But Solomon says, "The eyes of the LORD are everywhere, keeping watch on the wicked and the good" (Proverbs 15:3), which assures me that in His time and in His way, God will punish the wicked, the prideful and arrogant of heart.

51

But this passage also humbles me, for it forces me to realize that I too am unrighteous and that apart from God's grace and His mercy, I deserve punishment as well. This changes, or should change, my attitude toward others. Recognizing that I deserve full punishment for my wickedness, I desire to see my friends who do not live wisely know the graciousness and love that come from God. We are drawn to justice because it is central to God's character, but once we find Him, we realize we need His mercy and grace as well. His amazing grace and righteous judgment are a mystery that is wonderful to embrace. Acknowledging this should fuel our practice of justice with others to be "seasoned with salt" and "full of grace" (Colossians 4:6).

UNDERSTANDING RIGHT AND WRONG

Throughout Scripture, God is always very obvious when defining right and wrong. With the first humans He created, He simply gave them one command: "You are free to eat from any tree in the garden but you must not eat from the tree of the knowledge of good and evil, for when you eat of it, you will surely die" (Genesis 2:16). When He spoke to Moses for the benefit of the people of Israel, He gave Ten Commandments (see Exodus 20:1-17). When asked what was the Greatest Commandment, Jesus simply said that the entire Old Testament can be summed up as this: "Love the Lord your God with all your heart and with all your soul and with all your mind. . . . [And] love your neighbor as yourself" (Matthew 22:37-40). If we love God and others with the totality of our lives, it becomes much harder to do wrong.

In Romans 12:9, we are encouraged to "hate what is evil" and "cling to what is good." Paul's first letter to the Thessalonians encourages us to test everything, hold on to what is good, and avoid that which is evil (see 1 Thessalonians 5:21-22).

Knowing right from wrong is fundamental to having wisdom; living righteously is the key to living wisely.

The LORD detests lying lips, but he delights in men who are truthful. (Proverbs 12:22)

Honesty is central to everything we do. Once we lose our integrity, the right path has been compromised, our motives will always be in question, people will be hurt, and our witness for God will be significantly damaged. That is why honest words are so important to the Lord. Most of us have been victims of words spoken that were not true but did loads of damage. Sometimes we can be deceitful in the way we use our words so that they are true, but the meaning others hear is not. That is not pleasing to the Lord either. He desires for us to treat His creations fairly.

The first to present his case seems right, till another comes forward and questions him. (Proverbs 18:17)

When students come to me with difficulties regarding their parents, I often ask them, "What percentage of this problem is your parents', and what percentage is yours?" This immediately gets students thinking about the proportion of the issue that is their own responsibility. Interestingly, most students do not attribute the majority of the problem to their parents when asked!

It is amazing how two different people can see the same situation in completely different ways and both be convinced they are absolutely correct! The wise person always realizes there are several vantage points to an issue and carefully tries to understand all that is valid and not valid from each side.

53

What you have seen with your eyes do not bring hastily to court, for what will you do in the end if your neighbor puts you to shame? (Proverbs 25:7-8)

So often, we rush to take offense to others when really patience is needed to allow proper understanding to settle in. When we are offended, we are wise to take some time and really understand the situation and the case around it. Being hasty to bring matters to light can end in our own embarrassment. E-mail makes this easy. It is just too simple to write quickly and send instantly before we have time to truly consider a matter. In the old days, when I had to go to the trouble of writing and sending a letter, it gave time for me to carefully consider a matter. I can't count how many times I've wished I'd waited to push "send." Now I make it a habit to sit on a sensitive-issue e-mail for at least two hours before sending it. Sometimes after rereading the e-mail, I realize I am not being fair or clear and save myself from embarrassment.

Who can say, "I have kept my heart pure; I am clean and without sin"? (Proverbs 20:9)

The ability to determine right from wrong and to be fair to others is difficult work. What is so difficult in living a just life is that our own sin often makes us feel like hypocrites. *How can I possibly hold anyone to this standard when I myself struggle with it?* Ultimately, we need to remember that God is the only one who judges motivations of the heart. If God never changes, then right and wrong do not change, although our comprehension of them may.

54

Jesus was gracious to those who lived with a bit of sincerity. It was those who were being condemned by others whom He forgave and asked to go away and sin no more. Jesus held the standard and never slacked on wrong, yet He was also kind and loving to those who were lost in their wrongdoing. His actions repelled hypocrites (Pharisees) but attracted known sinners and outcasts. This is the essence of living justly. As people who deal with sin, it's important to remember that we have a gracious Savior, who forgives us just as much as those we struggle to forgive. So we shouldn't be afraid to confess our sin. For example, when sharing his faith with others, the apostle Paul didn't hide the fact that he used to kill Christians (see Acts 7:59–8:3; 1 Timothy 1:15). In the same way, our honesty about our own failings can further legitimize the power of God's grace and its transforming power in our lives.

THINK ABOUT IT

1. Think of a situation (like the Simpson trials) when justice seemed lost. How did you feel at the time? Why do you think you felt that way?

2. Read Romans 2:6-8. How do you respond to the idea that justice is personal to God and that He either delights in or is angry with people?

3. Read 1 Corinthians 3:10-15. How does understanding this passage's message make you a wiser person? How does it affect your motives and actions?

4. Describe the most fair-minded person you know. Is that person's life seasoned with grace and humility? How can you actively learn from that person?

5. What are some differences between focusing on the benefits of salvation in evangelism and focusing on God's supreme justice? How would a deeper understanding of God's justice help a new believer trust God more? How would it help you?

56

6. Which stage (child, adolescent, or adult) best represents your grasp of the wisdom of justice? Explain your answer.

WHAT'S IT WORTH?
UNDERSTANDING THE VALUE OF VALUES

People all over the world define their values differently. Usually those values are determined by a written code: the law, the Bible, the Quran, game rules, military codes. While some value the sanctity of life more than anything else, others value environmental protection. Some value money, still others value religion, and sometimes they value both together. Depending on where they look to learn these values, people can operate entirely different from one another.

As Christians, we determine our values through our knowledge of God, His Son, and His Word. Because values are a key element in becoming wise, we'll spend this chapter delving even deeper into God's heart and examining what matters most to Him.

THE STARTING POINT: STANDARDS

Standards tell us *what* is expected of us—the do's and don'ts. Values explain why we do them. Rules and guidelines are tremendously important, but the human heart longs for more. We long for meaning, purpose, and relationship. Standards remain intact; they are the boards that form the sides of the sandbox and give us boundaries for choices and behaviors. But values stimulate us to be creative, to love and laugh, to build and defend. Christians' values are rooted in our concept of God, and our sense of meaning is a reflection of our grasp of God's character.

I love Scriptures that describe the wonder of God's nature. Isaiah 6 depicts the prophet's vision of being in the throne room of God. The sight completely overwhelms him. The apostle John was probably Jesus' best friend on earth, but when the resurrected Christ appeared in a vision, John "fell at his feet as though dead" (Revelation 1:17). He fainted. In our day, we see God as our buddy. Yes, Jesus called us His friends, but we aren't peers. He is the One who spoke and a hundred billion galaxies were flung into space. He created the entire universe, and He didn't even sweat. We begin our search for meaning by looking with awe, reverence, and wonder at the God who created, sustains, judges, and cares for each of us. He owes us nothing; we owe Him everything. From that beginning point, we ask, *What, then, is important to God? Because what's important to God needs to be important to me.* That's the heart and soul of Christian values.

58 CONTRASTS

We humans think we're really smart. We think we've got it all figured out. When I walk by a magazine rack at the grocery store or large bookstore (who buys all of those, anyway?), I see what the world values. The most popular magazines tell me that great sex and being skinny are the two most important things in the universe. If I dig a little deeper and flip through the pages, I see only the young and beautiful in ads, and I see how to make a zillion dollars without working. Ads and articles promise that I can be popular and have prestige, money, and power if I buy this toothpaste and use that investment firm.

To clarify God's values and make them our own, we need to do some homework to identify the conflicting, nonstop messages we see and hear every day. Here are some thoughts on how God's values supersede those of the world:

- Our culture values youth; God values wisdom that comes with experience and age. (see Proverbs 16:31; 20:29)
- Our culture loves speed; God praises those who are patient. (see Proverbs 14:29)
- Our culture says possessions and wealth are the keys to happiness; God says a reputation for integrity and kindness is far more important. (see Proverbs 22:1; 14:31)
- Our culture promises that life should be full of passion and pleasure; God promises that hard work will be rewarded and that pleasure can destroy. (see Proverbs 14:23; 21:17)

I could go on and on, but you get the picture. A few years ago, George Barna wrote a book called *The Frog in the Kettle*.[1] His point was that Christian values are slowly eroding and with devastating consequences, much the same way a frog in a pot of water will remain, oblivious as the heat increases so much that soon he is cooked. Christian values are boiled in the slowly changing water around us, but do we even notice?

We can't do much about the culture, but we can do something about ourselves. And the first step is to recognize how the water is heating up. What do you find when you compare God's values with the world's values in ads, articles, sitcoms, movies, and conversations? When a friend of mine reads magazines or watches television or movies, he asks himself, *What's the real promise here?* In other words, what does the ad or story promise to provide? In most cases, this simple test exposes the ridiculous promises we hear and see all day, every day. The problem is that we don't test these things; we just believe them.

WHAT THE WORLD VALUES IN ADVERTISING

Here's a brief preview of current advertisements. In some ads, it's simple to see that their promises for a fuller life, such as the ability to have better sex or go on the right diet, are lacking. And unlike in the commercials where everyone is celebrating and happy, the beer we drink most likely won't get us the right friends or the right marriage partner. The car we drive might energize us a bit more, but if it costs more than our college education, our values are off. A recent trend—and one wholly subscribed to by much of college culture, at least—is wearing Abercrombie & Fitch clothing. Sure, it looks cool and is very durable, but the cost is outrageous and the company actually advertises all over its store walls using giant posters of naked people (ironically, they're not even wearing Abercrombie & Fitch clothes), usually suggesting casual sex with multiple partners. I'm not saying we should wear only clothes that don't "sell sex," for then we'd have nothing to wear, but sadly, many unwittingly accept Madame Folly's invitation or represent values that God definitely wouldn't value. And others unconsciously build their identity around the brands they choose to wear, drive, and adorn their house with.

60

VALUING APPROPRIATELY: COMMANDS, INTERPRETATIONS, AND OPINIONS

Some people "major on the minors." They're passionate about things that simply don't matter or miss the point entirely—for instance, the Pharisees not condoning healings on the Sabbath. Sports can be an obsession, especially for people who have "their team." I know people (and you know them too) whose moods are directly connected to the score of the last game or their fantasy sports stats. They are depressed or elated based on how their team did rather than on how they're doing with God. These activities should not carry such intense emotional importance in light of what really matters in life.

By making a distinction between commands, interpretations, and opinions, we can get a better idea of what's really important to God. That way we won't waste our time sweating the small stuff.

Commands (Essentials)

Commands are the truths we stand on that distinguish Christianity from other faiths. I admit that the word *command* is often viewed negatively in our culture, but Jesus used this word quite often. It's important because commands are essential to our "alignment," which we now know helps us develop wisdom.

He told us that if we love Him, we will obey His commands. He also told us in the Great Commission that we should make disciples of all nations, baptizing them and teaching them all that He commanded.

As I mentioned in the previous chapter, when it comes to commands, there are two that stand out, and those are the two Jesus claimed were most important: to love the Lord your God with everything you are, and to love your neighbor as yourself (see Matthew 22:37-40).

Interpretations (Culture)

Interpretations are the applications of God's Word. While there can be only one correct interpretation of Scripture, we may have different ways of applying this truth to our lives. And while I believe God has revealed one unified truth, our human minds often cannot see that truth clearly, so we have different interpretations of various passages based on our study. Often these views are shared within the context of culture and community. There are many laws that were given to the people of Israel in the Old Testament that are no longer significant in the context of our culture today. Understanding our culture and community makes our interpretations valid.

I grew up in California and spent quite a bit of time at the beach. Because of the beach culture, I grew up around members of the opposite sex in bathing suits, many people sporting a lot of flesh. Because of this, the standards of modesty were very different than they might have been in another part of the country. When I started working in youth ministries around the nation, I found it very odd that several camps didn't allow guys and girls to swim together. They called it "mixed bathing" (which makes swimming sound really creepy). I have to admit, I first thought these people were seriously backward until I realized that many came from small agricultural communities and that their standards of modesty were just different.

Another example: When I was visiting India, many young Christian men wanted to hold my hand as I walked down the street visiting with them. In their culture, this was totally appropriate, but the feelings I had inside were really uncomfortable.

In another country, the girls in our group could not understand why the missionaries asked them to refrain from wearing makeup. Not understanding the cultural interpretations of modesty, they ignored this instruction. On the train, they were shocked at how many men groped them as they passed by while the "unpainted" girls were untouched. In this area of the world, wearing makeup was something only prostitutes did.

In the United States, many Christian communities frown on alcohol consumption in any amount. While the Bible gives us strong commands against drunkenness, there are certain passages that could be applied in a way that allows for Christians to drink. My brother Jeremy was surprised when in Ireland the pastor took him to a pub to have a pint with the deacons and other church members the night before my brother was to speak in church. So it's easy to see that because different communities have different interpretations of what is appropriate, it's important that we consider Scripture in the context of history and culture. That way, our interpretations produce wisdom beyond our limited cultural environment.

Opinions (Personal Choices)

Opinions are personal inclinations that don't carry the same weight as commands or interpretations. It doesn't matter whether you like pepperoni or Italian sausage on your pizza, how many levels of angels you believe exist in heaven, or even what presidential candidate you vote for (although many might argue that fits best in the "interpretations" category). Most of these are simply not worth getting into an argument over.

63

Because of my personal opinions about Scripture and how I believe I should pursue holiness in my life, I may choose to live differently than other Christians. Many of my opinions are not worth imposing on or even discussing with others. My opinions might help me live for Christ more effectively, but someone else might not have the same concerns. Paul writes, "Whether you eat or drink or whatever you do, do it all to the glory of God" (1 Corinthians 10:31).

Problems, of course, come from two directions. Some people

are too passionate, and some aren't passionate enough. A friend of mine returned from a Spring Break trip with a cross tattooed on his arm. Another friend just couldn't believe the guy would do such a thing. A tattoo. It always came up, and eventually it fractured their relationship. But I also know people who don't have a clue what they believe, so they don't bother to have opinions.

So commands, interpretations, and opinions help us develop our values. What matters to God and to us is based on the commands of God's Word, which are the bedrock of faith and choices. Our interpretations grow out of those commands. And opinions—ours and others'—can be sources of learning and going deeper into our interpretations of God's commands.

TESTING OUR VALUES

College is a fantastic time to challenge your values. Questioning your faith and convictions is a normal, healthy part of the learning experience. Some will find their faith is weak or only borrowed from their parents. College may be the time to develop their very own faith. Others may realize that the things they cherished are as strong as a rock. In either case, the process of questioning, listening, watching, and reflecting can clarify values.

Jesus always welcomed questions from a sincere inquirer, but don't expect to have all your questions answered as a freshman. Challenging your commands, interpretations, and opinions will take you into the mud and confusion of conflicting ideas, but that's not a tragedy at all. Go, wade in, and find people who can wrestle with you. Like the guide in John Bunyan's *The Pilgrim's Progress*,[2] you can select people to accompany you on your wisdom journey, and they can help you take new steps that help strengthen your faith.

THINK ABOUT IT

1. Read Isaiah 6:1-8 and Revelation 1:12-18. Why is it important to begin with God's awesome character to define your values?

2. Make a list of five to ten of your favorite ads or commercials, and then answer these questions for each one: What is the implied promise? What does the ad say the product or service will do for you?

3. What percentage of the time are you exposed to the world's values (around your friends, in class, in ads, in films)? What percentage of the time are you focused on God's values? What do these numbers say about the input you are receiving? How is it affecting your life?

4. How comfortable are you with testing your values to see what you really believe? What do you need to help you in this process?

5. Aligning your values with God's requires surrender. Describe what this surrender looks and feels like. What are some reasons you may resist surrendering? What are some ways you can overcome resistance in your own life?

SQUINTING IN FOG:
THE MYSTERY OF GOD'S WISDOM

> *We don't yet see things clearly. We're squinting in a fog,*
> *peering through a mist. But it won't be long before the weather*
> *clears and the sun shines bright! We'll see it all then, see it*
> *all as clearly as God sees us, knowing him directly just as he*
> *knows us!* (1 Corinthians 13:12, MSG)

We face two main kinds of mystery: the wonder of God's creation and the confusion of not comprehending His will. Both are parts of the Christian experience, and both play important roles in deepening our faith and making us wiser people. Usually confusion about God, more than other types of mystery, can make us feel frustrated, like we're looking through a dusty window wearing unfocused glasses. It's a good thing that God gave us His Holy Spirit, His Word, and His patience.

THE WONDER OF GOD'S CREATION

The Hubble telescope is one of the greatest advances in the history of astronomy. First used in 1990, it's named after the astronomer Edwin Hubble, who in 1923 discovered that the universe goes beyond our own galaxy. With the telescope's incredible power, scientists are observing wonders far beyond anything they'd imagined only a few years ago. The distances, sizes, and varieties of stars in the universe are staggering, but really, unless we happen to be rocket scientists, we're not given much opportunity to study stars ourselves. But no matter how incredibly immense the universe is, God is bigger. Isaiah told us that God marks off the heavens "with the breadth of his hand" (Isaiah 40:12), which is the distance between the end of the little finger and the thumb when the hand is stretched out. This is a poetic way of saying that all of creation is very manageable to our infinite God. He holds it all in His hand.

The mystery of space and time is pretty impressive. The mystery of human life might be even more impressive. As researchers learn more about the human body, our amazement at its complexity multiplies. In each cell of our bodies, we find the building blocks of life: DNA. The human genome consists of a long strand with two filaments. These filaments are wound so tightly into a double helix that if the DNA from a single cell were stretched, it would be over five feet long. But that strand is incredibly narrow, only fifty-trillionths of an inch wide. Dr. Richard Swenson tells us that all of the DNA from a human body could be compressed into an ice cube but that if each cell's DNA were stretched end to end, they would reach at least ten billion miles.[1]

68

The human brain is the most complex and sophisticated thing ever created. The "hardware" consists of ten billion neurons, each with thousands of connectors to other neurons, called *dendrites*. An electrical impulse travels over a connection, or synapse, as a chemical message. The brain has the capacity to hold one quintillion (that's 1,000,000,000,000,000,000) bits of information, one thousand times that of a supercomputer. (Then why do I have trouble remembering where I put my keys?) And I haven't even touched on the details of human cells, because, in fact, scientists are finding new and vaster domains at the molecular level.

To consider all the wonder of God's creation, the mystery of that which we cannot fully understand, is a wise venture in itself. It is wise to worship, filled with awe, a God who is smarter, wiser, and more complicated than any strand of DNA or any celestial universe.

THE FRUSTRATING MYSTERY OF GOD'S WILL

It's one thing to be okay with not comprehending the mystery of God's creation. I mean, God's creation functions without any input from us whatsoever. But when we're considering God's will, the will we seek when making decisions, it can be pretty frustrating. Sooner or later in each of our lives, God's direction and calling won't fit neatly into our plans or desires. Sometimes the mystery of God's will is not in lacking knowledge about God's desires for us but instead in wondering why in the world He would choose *that* plan for us. In those frustrating moments, it's easy to throw up our hands and blame God for not making sense to us. But when those times come, as difficult as it is to see past our flaring emotions, it's wise to practice discipline and dig deeper into God's character and purposes.

69

Perhaps the first step is to simply acknowledge that God's will is always far bigger and more complex than we can imagine. It's really a matter of perspective. God created us—the whole world and everything in it—so He probably has a slight advantage on our scope of understanding. Isaiah recorded God's reminder to us:

"For my thoughts are not your thoughts,
neither are your ways my ways," declares the LORD.
"As the heavens are higher than the earth,

so are my ways higher than your ways
and my thoughts than your thoughts." (Isaiah 55:8-9)

Some of us, though, are intellectually dishonest. First, we refuse to read this passage in its context and instead spout it off as a way to "prove our theology is right." That verse is not there for us to create our own knowledge of God or to defend a view that seems logically contradictory. Rather, it is to show that God's ways of giving grace are not like our ways. And He gives us grace (if we ask for it humbly) even after we've thrown temper tantrums at Him for not understanding His will.

The second step in embracing the mystery of God's will is to begin valuing tough questions, even if we don't get clear answers. Many think Isaiah 55:8-9 allows us to refrain from asking hard questions. We might say, "God's ways are too big for me, so I'm not even going to try to understand, because God's ways are higher than mine." Often we're afraid of the answers or we've been taught that it's wrong to ask. Some of us are more comfortable with simple, clear answers. Often when the easy answers don't work, we bury our heads in the sand. Simple formulas make us feel more secure, more comfortable.

A HABIT OF CHILDLIKE OR CHILDISH FAITH?

William Lane Craig, in his book *Hard Questions, Real Answers*,[2] distinguishes between childish faith and childlike faith. Childish faith is using "blind faith" as a crutch whenever questions get tough and answers aren't easy. Childlike faith, on the other hand, is an eagerness to learn and ask questions; it's a sincere desire for answers yet a trust in a higher source. It realizes we are "seeing as a poor reflection in the mirror" (see 1 Corinthians 13:12), even in our interpretation and application of Isaiah 55:8-9.

I have many times fallen into the trap of using the Isaiah passage in a childish way, mostly because it developed as a habit early in life. It's important that we don't replace childlike faith with childish faith.

Although it may seem oxymoronic, making childlike faith our habit will actually increase our wisdom. Habits save time and energy. Mental and spiritual habits allow us to trust God and pursue truth instead of practicing foolishness and naivete.

We are not called to be spiritual pygmies, unwilling or unable to cope with ambiguities. Those who grow deep in the Lord, who gain wisdom, and who then are able to help others through life's inevitable difficulties are those who have the courage to be intellectually honest and say those three wonderful words: "I don't know." That admission, however, is not an excuse for fatalism and passivity. We are still compelled to grope for answers that lie outside our comfortable boxes.

THIS IS THE WILL OF GOD?

A host of authors have written powerfully about the mystery of God's will. Philip Yancey's *Disappointment with God*[3] is a classic I recommend if and when you go through strange, mysterious times. I also suggest the biblical saga of Job, which depicts a man whose experience made no sense to him or his friends. Many of us can relate. Job was confused, distressed, and heartbroken by the suffering—needless, unexplainable suffering—he endured. He reflected:

Yet when I hoped for good, evil came;
    when I looked for light, then came darkness.
The churning inside me never stops;
    days of suffering confront me. (Job 30:26-27)

A trusted friend betrays us (Job's friends betrayed him repeatedly with their terrible advice about God's will and ways, and later God chastised them). A tragic accident claims the life of a family member or close friend. A professor grades us unfairly, and we lose our scholarship. Gnawing pain and shame well up from sexual or physical abuse. Our parents' marriage is shattered by infidelity. A grandparent slides into the abyss of Alzheimer's. The lab report comes back, and it's terminal cancer. These and a thousand other problems shake up our world and make us feel like Job. For some of us, these tragedies are completely unexpected, and we think, *How can this be the will of God?* All of us confront this kind of dilemma from time to time, but for others, the pain of a shattered life is constant, daily, never-ending. Job's losses were both sudden and complete. He suffered the deaths of his children, the destruction of all he owned, and a debilitating disease of painful boils all over his body. All he had left was his complaining wife and three condemning friends.

In times of darkness and mystery, the law of sowing and reaping is suspended. Bad things happen to good people, and we look around and notice that many who don't give a rip about God are doing great. This ethical problem is as old as the writer of Job and as fresh as today's news. It's summed up like this: If God is good, surely He wouldn't allow suffering; therefore, there must be some limitation of His sovereign power to secure goodness for His people. And if God has complete, sovereign power over everything, suffering surely shows that He doesn't care that bad things happen to good people, so He's not good. But the mental, emotional, and spiritual struggle for us in the face of a crisis is not a philosophical debate. An answer to the question "How can this be the will of God?" is intensely personal and necessary for our survival. Our agony, like Job's, is very real, very current, and very devastating.

In his commentary on the book of Job, Francis I. Anderson clarifies this dilemma:

> *Evil is not always—not often!—punished in proportion to guilt; good is not always—not often!—rewarded in proportion to merit. The case of Job precipitates the test of faith in its severest form: the supremely righteous man who sustains the most extreme calamities. How can he, or anyone, continue to believe that God is right and fair in what He sometimes does to people? There can be no doubt that it is God, only God, who is responsible for all that happens to Job. It cannot be blamed on "Nature" or the Devil, for these are but His creatures.*[4]

Job asks many questions, but God never condemns him for asking them. Some might give up and say, "Ours is not to reason why. Ours is but to do or die," but God says (ironically also in Isaiah) to us, "Come now, let us reason together" (1:18). God is not surprised or offended by our questions. On several matters that were within human comprehension, God laid out His arguments for His ways. Although God does not explain Himself on every issue, we come to understand that God is not arbitrary or random in the way He has created the universe or in the requirements He places on human life. God is a God of reason and can defend Himself if He chooses. He invites questions because they show we are pursuing Him.

IN TIMES OF DARKNESS

St. John of the Cross describes times when God seems to be absent as "the dark night of the soul."[5] We pray, but there's no answer. We read the Scriptures, but the words make no sense. We try to talk to someone and get help, but the person doesn't understand. I hope you aren't going through darkness and confusion today, but someday you will. When that happens to you, you can learn some of life's richest lessons. And when it happens to someone you love, you can help with insight and comfort.

Typically when I have gone through these periods of darkness (one might actually call them spiritual "numbness"), I have emerged with a deeper understanding of my spiritual walk. But it took months and sometimes years to discern what God was possibly doing. It is important to remain faithful to God during these times, even when we feel He is absent. This can be valued only through wisdom and can be accomplished only when we are in proper alignment with God.

Perhaps one of the most damaging things we can do when going through spiritual confusion is to abandon wisdom. If we hope to make it out safely to the other side of the valley, we need to be guided by wisdom—to be disciplined to discern the deep and subtle cause-and-effect relationships around us, to remember what God requires (humble and right living), and to value what God values (faith). Hebrews 11 is a "hall of faith," but it required much wisdom and discipline for those people to be mentioned on that list.

JOSEPH AS A MODEL FOR SEEING
THE WISDOM IN MYSTERY

Think about how both Josephs embraced mystery while straining to be wise. The New Testament Joseph was told by his fiancée that she was pregnant from the Holy Spirit. Sounds like the worst excuse for unfaithfulness I've heard. But with patience, trust, and the help of God's guidance through dreams, he decided to endure the shame of marrying a woman who was already pregnant.

The Old Testament Joseph was given what he thought was a good dream from God, but by failing to discern the consequences of sharing it with his brothers and interpret their views of justice and values beforehand, he soon found himself sold as a slave. Even when he did the right thing, such as avoiding sleeping with his boss's wife, he found himself in prison. But he trusted God, despite God giving him little reason to. Funny how Scripture describes a person living with the right attitude despite horrible circumstances as having the Lord with him and given "success in whatever he did" (Genesis 39:23). This surely isn't the world's way of valuing success, but it was success to God. God's success often includes suffering; Joseph and Job are painful examples. Eventually, after many years, Joseph saw God's plan to turn what his brothers meant for evil into good (see Genesis 50:20) when he saved their lives during a wretched famine (see Genesis 47:13-27). Joseph again looked beyond the fog and sought discernment through this mystery. The result was inclusion in the Hebrews hall of faith.

When we encounter dark times, our emotions explode and cloud our ability to practice the skill of wisdom. To sustain us, we need friends, mentors, and the habit of relating honestly to God. In those times, don't quit. Ask questions. Cling to what you already know, and dig deeper into the character of God. But remember your human limitations in understanding everything as God does. Passages about suffering that you've skipped over before (like Joseph's) may now mean far more to you. Find someone who won't give you simple, easy answers, and listen carefully as that person shares his or her heart.

God is the Creator, the One who is infinitely wise, whose purposes are far above ours. He is willing to use anything—absolutely anything—to teach us the deepest lessons in wisdom. He has a purpose for the dark times as well as the light, for there are seasons for every event in life (see Ecclesiastes 3:18). A wise person embraces this with childlike faith.

THINK ABOUT IT

1. In what ways does the study of astronomy and anatomy increase your sense of wonder and stimulate your faith?

2. Why is *wonder* an important part of *wisdom*? What would wisdom be lacking without wonder?

3. In your own words, define and describe *childish faith* and *childlike faith*.

4. Why did God allow Job to suffer so terribly? Did His reason seem just? What does this tell you about God's values as compared to ours?

5. What are some reasons people don't want to wrestle with difficult questions? Do any of these reasons match yours? If they do, explain your answer.

6. Have you ever experienced times of darkness as this chapter describes? If so, can you identify any cause?

7. Are times of darkness inevitable for every believer? Why or why not?

8. How would you encourage a friend who is going through a very difficult time and can't figure out why?

SPEED BUMPS:
OBSTACLES THAT MAKE OR BREAK WISDOM

As we've seen from the last chapter, the path to wisdom can feel like a treacherous road. In order to make wisdom work, in order to live wisdom and not just know what it is, there are certain skills we should master. Just as Danielson from the movie *The Karate Kid* had to spend hours practicing skills he wasn't sure were worth his time, without even realizing it we often are practicing life as a means for cultivating wisdom.

Life is God's tool. In order to be willing to be shaped by God, we must first recognize *how* He shapes us. Sometimes He creates obstacles that slow us down to help us grow before we can advance. They are kind of like speed bumps in the road. From one perspective, speed bumps can be a nuisance, but from another, we see they are placed or used by wise architects and road engineers for specific purposes—our "best" progress.

Remembering Joseph, Job, and Jesus, we can see that God's values are often not ours. The three "speed bumps" discussed in this chapter are *waiting, forgiving*, and *failing*. Though common, they are handled differently by each of us. They can either help us live wisely or lead us down the path of folly.

OBSTACLE OR TOOL #1: WAITING

We hate to wait. And we live around family, friends, and neighbors who also hate to wait. Any kind of delay is annoying. In fact, we've orchestrated our entire culture to avoid having to wait. We bank where we can get in and out in a flash, or we bank online. We scan the lines at checkout counters and moan if we get in "the wrong line" and are delayed by a couple of minutes. We are thrilled with our new computer speed—until the next, faster generation hits the shelves. Young Americans think that waiting is maybe the worst thing that can happen to them. That's too bad, though, because God sees it very differently. It's one of His tools.

Lessons from Homemade Ice Cream

I've learned some important lessons about waiting by making ice cream. Call me crazy, but I didn't like homemade ice cream when I was a kid. It was always too mushy, and it fell off the spoon before I could get it to my mouth. However, when Jade and I had kids, we thought, *If we don't make ice cream for Dax and Skye, they'll grow up thinking we're communists or something.* But I was determined to find a new way to make better ice cream.

I looked through some recipe books and read something that dramatically improved the course of civilization—or at least my ability to make ice cream. The best recipes call for letting the ingredients rest. I'd never heard this before. How do you let your ingredients rest? The idea is simply to put your mixed ingredients in the refrigerator for six to twelve hours *before* putting them in the ice cream maker. The process of waiting does something magnificent to the mixture, and the taste is far smoother and richer. This requires planning ahead. To get the ice cream firmer, let it harden in the freezer after it's made rather than serving it right out of the maker.

The lesson is clear: if I want mushy, tasteless ice cream, I can rush the process and get it done quickly, but if I want something rich and wonderful, I have to wait. The time spent in waiting isn't a *hindrance* to fulfilling my goal; it is *instrumental* in fulfilling my goal. That's how God sees it too.

"I Want It Now"

We want it all, and we want it now. We're in a hurry to find the best friends in the world, the mate who will love us for the rest of our lives, and a great job where we'll spend fifty to sixty hours a week for the next forty years. We look around at all the people who seem to have those things now and we think, *Hey, why not me?*

In my opinion, a majority of poor decisions occur because we hurry to make a decision. We compare our situations with the best ones around and suddenly feel pressure to make changes. I know a girl who watched four of her closest girlfriends get engaged by their senior year of college—all but this girl. She was really happy for her friends, and they often invited this girl to go along with them out to dinner or to parties. She appreciated that, but because she wasn't engaged, she felt more and more excluded from their excitement. By February of their senior year, she was tired of waiting. She wanted her ring too. She started dating guys she wouldn't have looked at twice before, and soon one of them expressed more than casual interest. *Then* she felt better about herself. *Then* she had something to talk to her friends about.

The guy asked her to marry him, but she was shocked when her friends told her she was crazy for even thinking about it. She was furious. Why couldn't she enjoy all that they enjoyed? Tempers cooled, and that summer, all five couples married. A year later, this young woman filed for divorce. She was broken and devastated by her rush to have a relationship like those of her friends. Her desire for approval and acceptance, and the incorrect view that marriage would "complete her" all manifested themselves in impatience and frustration at having to wait.

God's Purposes in Waiting

God is eternal. He sees the end from the beginning, so waiting is no big deal to Him. Second Peter 3:8 points out that "with the Lord a day is like a thousand years, and a thousand years are like a day." It's no wonder that it can be His tool yet our obstacle. His purposes for us are good, but His path is often much different than what we'd choose. We want the tasty, hardened ice cream now, but God knows that unless we wait, we won't fully experience His gifts to us.

The first thing we have to get through our skulls is that waiting is God's way of shaping our motives and preparing us for the future. If we resist it, we only hinder God's work in accomplishing His purposes, and we cause more delays. When we are forced to wait for an answer to prayer or a solution to a problem, whether we like it or not, we are more dependent on God's work in us. Lady Wisdom asks, "Lord, why are you taking so long? Is there something you or I need to do to prepare me for this answer?" The answer to that question is almost always yes. During the delay, God might tap us on the shoulder and show us motives that are off base, but this isn't always His approach. When Job waited weeks for the answer to why he was suffering, God was silent, and in the end He never even answered the question. As C. S. Lewis warns us in *A Grief Observed*,[1] testing and patience often reveal to us whether our faith was just a "house of cards"—or as Jesus says, whether the house was built on sand or solid rock (see Matthew 7:24-26).

Maybe we wanted something great to happen and didn't realize that our hidden motive was so other people would think highly of us, or the thought that God should always bless us to make our lives easy. Selfish motives can be excused or rationalized very easily, but waiting has a way of surfacing those motives.

Sometimes we have to wait because God is preparing other people or a situation. We might think, *It's not fair for God to make me wait just because somebody else is slow.* I remember a couple who got engaged but the girl's mom didn't approve. The guy wisely told the mother, "I love your daughter, but I do not want to get married without your blessing. You are too important in our lives. I am willing to wait until you have a change of heart or God leads us in other directions." The mom was thrilled to know her power. But over the next year, God took her through some extraordinary life events that eventually left her broken. Her response eventually was, "Please get married, I am sorry that my selfishness has caused you such pain." God's purposes are far bigger and broader than ours, and He is the sovereign Lord who knows exactly what He's doing. The Christian faith isn't a democracy; God is a benevolent King. He does what is good and right to accomplish His divine purposes, even if it's inconvenient for us.

83

Waiting deepens our dependence on God. When life moves fast, it's easy to coast in our relationship with Him. Delay forces us to analyze what we really believe about God and His purposes for our lives. Through the process of trusting God, we find the pearl of God's majesty. Eventually, the wise realize more deeply than ever that He is good, He is sovereign over all things, and His will is inscrutable. I'm convinced that God cares far more about our faith than our success and comfort—and it is in the furnace of waiting that our faith is melted, purified, and reformed.

Crying Out for God

I've heard a lot of Christian leaders say that waiting on God is one of the most difficult things they've ever done. When we're impatient with God, we're in good company. Psalms is the songbook of the Bible, but not everything in the psalms is upbeat and happy. The writers express honest, sometimes gut-wrenching emotions. In the first two verses of one painful psalm, David pours out his frustration at waiting. Four times in the two verses, David anguishes, "How long, O LORD? Will you forget me forever?" (Psalm 13:1). And that's our songbook.

The answer may not be what you want, and God's timing may not be on your schedule, but when He is ready, He'll do what He knows is best. I love the proverbs because they communicate truth so clearly. One that speaks to our difficulty with delay is Proverbs 13:12: "Hope deferred makes the heart sick, but a longing fulfilled is a tree of life." When you experience delays, don't let your heart become too sick. Disappointment is understandable, but don't give up on God. Realize that waiting is just as much a part of God's eternal, perfect purpose for your life as the most instant answer to prayer. And in fact, you won't become the person God wants you to be if you despise the chisel of delay that's in His hands. Instead, let it be a tool for wisdom in your life.

OBSTACLE OR TOOL #2: FORGIVING

Some of the wisest people I know are those who give and receive forgiveness. Conversely, some of the most foolish people I know are those who hold on to bitterness that ruins their lives and poisons their relationships. A wise person has the heart and courage to forgive. It takes both.

In many ways, the first year of college is a vulnerable time for most of us. It's an adventure, for sure, but adventures involve risks. One of the risks we take in college is that we open ourselves up and that can lead to hurt. In a few cases, demanding, domineering people actually intend to hurt us so we'll cower under their power. But in the vast majority of cases, hurts are a result of misunderstandings, miscommunication, and misguided expectations. We are like a herd of porcupines bumping up against each other, sticking each other whether we mean to or not.

Experience and Expression — Learning from Peter

An important principle of forgiveness is that we can't give away something we don't possess. Paul wrote to the Ephesians, "Be kind and compassionate to one another, forgiving each other, just as in Christ God forgave you" (Ephesians 4:32). Did you get that? We are to forgive others out of our own experience of being forgiven by Christ. To put it another way, the degree of our willingness and ability to *express* forgiveness to those who hurt us is directly proportional to our own *experience* of Christ's forgiveness of our sins. If we aren't willing to forgive others, then we first need to focus on our own depravity and God's great grace toward us. As the reality of Christ's sacrifice for our sins sinks in, we'll be more willing to forgive others who offend us.

85

The story of Peter's denial and Jesus' forgiveness is a wonderful reminder of the scope of God's grace. Peter's three denials on the night Jesus was arrested didn't come as a shock to Jesus, even though Peter had previously insisted that he was willing to lay down his life (see Matthew 26:35; John 13:37). We can only imagine the great sorrow and guilt that Peter felt during the arrest and Crucifixion.

But after Jesus rose again, He appeared to the disciples and singled out Peter for special attention. Peter's knees were probably shaking. It must have been worse than being called in to see the dean. As a painful parallel to Peter's three denials, Jesus asked him three times, "Peter, do you love me?" (see John 21:15-17). The fisherman's affirmations were his acceptance of Christ's gracious offer of forgiveness, and Peter's life was never the same again; he had experienced true forgiveness. His sin caused him tremendous pain and confusion, but Christ's forgiveness healed his heart. That's a wonderful picture of Christ's forgiveness for you and me too.

The Joys of Bitterness

In an article in *Christianity Today*,[2] author Philip Yancey called forgiveness "the unnatural act." Human nature wants revenge. Our instincts drive us to make people pay for what they've done to us. Anger is a reasonable response to injustice, and others' sins against us are clearly a form of injustice. But if anger isn't resolved, it turns into bitterness. Many of us actually thrive on bitterness. Yes, I know that sounds odd, but bitterness provides two essentials that make us feel alive: identity and energy. When we've been wronged, we can cling to that offense and define ourselves as "the victim," "the one who got the shaft." And we wake up every day with a little more fire to get that person back and to never, ever let anyone else hurt us.

In his brief and brilliant book *Wishful Thinking*,[3] Frederick Buechner wrote about the effects of bitterness:

> *Of the Seven Deadly Sins, anger is possibly the most fun. To lick your wounds, to smack your lips over grievances long past, to roll over your tongue the prospect of bitter confrontations to come, to savor to the last toothsome morsel*

both the pain you are given and the pain you are giving
back—in many ways it is a feast fit for a king. The chief
drawback is that what you are wolfing down is yourself.
The skeleton at the feast is you.

We have lots of excuses for not forgiving those who have hurt us. Here are a few of the most common ones:

- He's not sorry he did it.
- It is too big to forgive.
- She needs to learn a lesson.
- I can't trust that he won't hurt me again.
- I just don't want to forgive. My anger feels justified.
- If I forgive her, I'll have to be nice to her, and I sure don't want to do that.

Make no mistake: forgiving a person who has hurt us is an unnatural act. It takes courage to fight through our instinct for revenge. That's why we need to experience Christ's forgiveness deeply to follow His example. After all, He went to the cross when He knew exactly what we were going to do and when we weren't sorry for what we did.

During my senior year in high school, a guy moved to town and came to our church. We soon became good friends, and I helped him fit in with the Christian group at school. That year, I decided to run for student body president, but to my surprise, this guy decided to run against me. That wasn't so bad, but during the campaign, this guy's key supporters did some underhanded, sleazy things to hurt me. (Just to be clear, the guy running against me had nothing to do with this.)

I confronted his two supporters and also went to the school administration, but they didn't do anything. I then told the administration, "Whether I win or lose, I want to file a protest right now about the way I've been treated." I lost the election by a few votes, and man, I was hacked. I felt it had been stolen from me.

During my first year of college, my anger at those two and the administration surfaced again (it hadn't been buried too far), and I knew I had to deal with it because it was really eating at me. My bitterness poisoned my heart and my relationships. I've always enjoyed humor, but before I forgave these two and the school administration, my humor became dark and negative. I was unhappy, and I was making people around me unhappy too.

One of the most important insights I've ever had was to realize that forgiving those who hurt me did far more to help me than to help the ones I forgave. Thoughts of revenge or avoiding that person absorbed my thoughts. My stomach was upset and my head hurt, but the person who hurt me either didn't know or didn't care. But gaining the courage to forgive was like leaving a cage. I was free to stop obsessing about that person and could then use my mental energy for understanding life from God's perspective (living wisely) instead of harboring anger against the injustice. Now I could move forward with my wisdom journey; I could finally overcome the obstacle.

Steps to Take

If you're alive, you're going to be hurt and you're going to hurt others. That's the nature of this life until we die. Denying, minimizing, or excusing these wounds doesn't resolve them. The first step is to be honest about them. If others have hurt us, we need to say, "Lord, that hurts. Help me deal with this in a way that honors You." One of David's psalms records that he actually asked for God to destroy his enemies and their wives, children, and ancestors. That's honest prayer. But simply speaking a prayer is easier than when the Holy Spirit taps us on the shoulder and shows us that we have offended someone and we need to say those three little words, "I was wrong."

Forgiveness doesn't come easily for any of us, so the next step is to go back to the Cross and reflect on Christ's wonderful grace in our own lives. Then, with our hearts full of thankfulness, we can choose to forgive those who have hurt us or go to those we have offended and ask for their forgiveness. We might or might not feel great relief when we give and receive forgiveness, but we know that ultimately we have most certainly gained wisdom.

OBSTACLE OR TOOL #3: FAILING

One of the most important things my dad taught his sons was not to be afraid of failure. He wanted us to be both bold and wise, and he knew we wouldn't be either if we were afraid to fail.

To some of us, failure is such a threat that we are driven to be sure it never happens to us. And others live passively under a cloud of constant shame and self-doubt because of past failures. It might have been only one event at a party, an entire year of high school rebellion, or not living up to your parents' or your own standards, but now the result of bad decisions and attitudes is constant torment.

One of the most important pieces of wisdom we can learn in college is to see failure as an opportunity instead of a threat. We think of Thomas Edison as one of the most successful inventors of all time, but he failed far more frequently than he succeeded. For every successful invention, Edison experienced tens of thousands of bombs.[4] Through his experiences, he learned to see failure as a stepping-stone instead of a roadblock. And Thomas Watson, Sr., the man who launched IBM, once said, "The fastest way to succeed is to double your failure rate."[5] Strange as it may sound, our ability to live wisely might depend heavily on how willing we are to forgive ourselves for failing in order to be willing to risk failure again.

Don't Fail with Failure

Those who are driven to avoid failure at all costs use two different methods. Some don't attempt anything that includes any risk at all. They are like a trial lawyer who has never lost a case but whose success rate is so high because he never takes a case that isn't a sure thing. Others are willing to take risks but micromanage every step to control the outcome. Still others aren't driven to avoid failure but are devastated by past failures and are susceptible to the temptations of self-pity. Passivity, however, prevents them from moving forward in learning, growing, and taking responsibility.

Some Christians are confused by failure because they think that if they are following God's leading and practicing wisdom, they'll surely succeed. In fact, they believe God has guaranteed their success. When they fail, they become introspective, wondering what hidden sin has displeased God, or they blame God for not being faithful. But God never promised a smooth path to success for any of us, including Jesus Himself. And even a casual reading of the lives of Moses, David, Paul, Peter, and many others in the Bible shows many failures. In addition, God often took those people into incredibly difficult times even though they earnestly sought His will—because difficult times are sometimes squarely in the middle of God's will.

Both the driven and the devastated need to see risk as a part of life. The question is not how to avoid all risks but how to learn from our risks. That's where wisdom plays a vital role. Elijah should have learned from his risk with the Baal worshipers that God's power is great, but instead when news came that Jezebel wanted to take his life, he immediately ran off into the wilderness and asked to die instead of learning to trust God when adversity struck (see 1 Kings 19:3-4). Quite often, taking the time to ask good questions and find their answers is all we need to help us take reasonable risks and enjoy a large measure of success.

Elijah learned to trust God more and went on to become one of the more memorable prophets in the Bible. But trust wasn't something he learned after only one try. He needed persistence and tenacity. We may recognize that we didn't ask the right questions at the beginning, or we may find out that a person we trusted didn't come through. Whatever the cause of the failure, we are wise to analyze it and continually try to learn from it so we don't fail in the same way again. Solomon failed repeatedly and eventually had to learn not to take himself and his decisions too seriously. As he stated,

91

> *A man can do nothing better than to eat and drink and find satisfaction in his work. This too, I see, is from the hand of God, for without him, who can eat or find enjoyment? To the man who pleases him, God gives wisdom, knowledge and happiness. (Ecclesiastes 2:24-26)*

Did you get that? God gives wisdom to those who are good in His sight. Does that mean those who are perfect? If David is a man after God's own heart and people like Elijah forget to trust

God a few hours after witnessing one of the most spectacular supernatural events in history, then this can't be what the passage means. Learning from our failures is the key for us to be good in His sight. And what is the result? Wisdom, knowledge, happiness, and the ability to tell yourself that your labor is good.

TOUGH AND TENDER

I've known a number of wonderful people who became terribly depressed in college. For some, being away from their parents' consistent support left them vulnerable. For others, terrible decisions wrecked their lives, and they didn't seek God's forgiveness and love to help them get out of their hole. And others simply couldn't measure up to unrealistically high expectations of academics, friends, and the Lord—yes, too high of expectations from God. The college experience is a test of virtually every aspect of life. For example, asking a girl or guy out on a date may be something we are too afraid of, and being vulnerable with friends may seem too unsafe. But if we maintain this fear and passivity, we prevent God from working in our lives through others to heal us.

Understand the pressures you feel; reflect on their causes and effects in your life and the lives of others. Some are a natural part of the college experience, but some may be unnatural, crushing pressures to be more and do more than you possibly can. Develop a heart that is both tender and tough—tender in sensitively listening to God's call to follow Him through thick and thin, but tough in clinging to the sovereignty and goodness of God through the dark times of failure as well as in the light of success.

It is critical to view failure as a tool and not an obstacle, have patience through the journey, and possess the courage to forgive yourself and others. If you don't, you will hinder progress in your journey more than you will accelerate it. What will you decide?

THINK ABOUT IT

1. Besides ice cream, what are some other things that are better if you wait for them? In each case, what would you lose if you didn't wait?

2. What are some ways God uses times of waiting to change your motives and deepen your dependence on Him? (How does He change your motives and help you trust Him more?)

3. Do you think you are more vulnerable to being hurt and hurting others during the first year or so of college than at other times in your life? Explain your answer.

4. Why is forgiveness an "unnatural act"?

5. What are some excuses you've used to keep from forgiving those who have offended you?

6. How do you normally respond to failure (driven to avoid it, devastated by it, wise in taking risks and learning from both success and failure)?

7. How does it affect your self-confidence and faith if you believe that God doesn't prevent your failures?

SECTION 2

ON THE ROAD:
LIVING WISELY AT
KEY CROSSROADS

HOW DO I LIVE WHAT I'VE LEARNED?

The first section of this book showed us the significance of alignment as it relates to the beginning of wisdom in our lives. Now that we've explored the three points of reference—cause and effect, justice, and values—and we understand how speed bumps are tools, not obstacles, in cultivating a deeper walk with God and others, let's see how to use them.

Most of the time, wisdom is developed over long periods of time as we experience and encounter many truths by observing life. This is why most of the images of wise people in our lives and in fantasy (for example, Gandalf and Yoda) are older. The beauty of understanding these truths is that they can actually accelerate our development of wisdom, allowing us to become wiser earlier in life. In Psalm 119:97-100, the poet writes,

> *Oh, how I love your law!*
> *I meditate on it all day long.*
> *Your commands make me wiser than my enemies,*
> *for they are ever with me.*
> *I have more insight than all my teachers,*
> *for I meditate on your statutes.*
> *I have more understanding than the elders,*
> *for I obey your precepts.*

God's Word gives us very profound yet seemingly simple insight into our everyday lives. Notice how the poet claims to have knowledge superior to that of his enemies, greater insight than learned people, and understanding without being "an old man."

In this section, I'll use specific passages of Scripture along with personal experiences to help you apply your new wisdom skills in some specific areas most freshmen wrestle with. Because Proverbs tells us that wisdom cannot be developed without a proper relationship with God, alignment is critical to this journey.

ALIGNMENT TO WHOSE WISDOM?

Earlier we discovered there are two types of wisdom: heavenly and worldly. It is powerful to contrast the types of questions God might want us to ask and what the world—infested by the "father of lies"—might want us to ask. Consider using the chart on the following page in any situation you encounter. The questions will help you discern whose invitation you might be pursuing.

Notice how self-centered the worldly questions are and how God-centered the heavenly ones are. The father of lies seeks to kill, steal, and destroy our ability to have life to the fullest, but he does it in a sneaky way. He gets us dwelling on it instead of dwelling on God. When we become preoccupied with ourselves, our pride is set loose, distracting us from finding what we are truly looking for: fulfillment.

In chapters 8–12, I'll encourage you to apply your newfound wisdom skills to the following topics: evaluating your faith, choosing friends, managing your time, relating to the opposite sex, and finding wisdom mentors.

Alignment Area	Heavenly	Worldly
Cause and Effect	Has God revealed what the consequences will be ahead of time?	Will it make me feel good?
	Who can help me discern what is going on around me from God's view?	Is this right for me?
Justice	Is this morally right to God?	Is it what I want?
	Am I treating others fairly?	What does society think?
Values	How much worth does God ascribe to this?	Will others think I'm important?
	Is this pursuit worthwhile to God?	How much worth do I give this?
Mystery/Speed Bumps	How does God want to use this in my life to help me grow?	This shouldn't be happening to me. Why is life so unfair?

BURSTING THE BUBBLE:
WHEN MY SPIRITUAL WORLD IS CHALLENGED, HOW WILL I RESPOND?

WHAT IS A BUBBLE?

When we start off for college, we begin a journey away from home and into ourselves. Whether we realize it or not, we embark on a journey outside of a bubble of beliefs we've been surrounded by. By *bubble*, I mean the combination of lectures from parents and pastors about what is right and wrong, the Sunday school flannel graphs that told us Bible-story truths (or VeggieTales for more modern kids) about God and Jesus and how He loves us, and the "because the Bible says so" answers of the faithful church attenders we've sat next to in church. In other words, the bubble is the aggregate of our beliefs and experiences that reinforce our beliefs.

The movie *Big Fish* portrays the pain and struggle of a son whose bubble has burst. At his father's deathbed, the son wants to show love to his father but can't forgive him for all the deceitful and distorted stories he heard as a child. Due to his anger at his own childhood naivete, he hadn't spoken to his dad in years and was unaware his father was terminally ill. The son's doubts and emotions are so strong that at times he explodes with rage when people believe and even enjoy these charming stories about his father's heroic accomplishments. In the emotional ending of the movie, he begins to find evidence that each story did have truthful elements to it and, although embellished, brought joy and wonder to the lives of all who could see it for its true value and worth.

Although I am not suggesting the Bible is an exaggerated story, *Big Fish* does illustrate how our beliefs are often tied to a very emotional part of our identity. When we begin to doubt the beliefs we inherited from our family and churches, the result can be a very painful process that can lead us toward or away from God's wisdom.

WHY WOULD A FRESHMAN'S BUBBLE BURST?

Within two months of our first year of college, we are flooded with new experiences, ideas, and perspectives. In a short time, we have met so many people, with so many different experiences than our own, that our bubble starts to get pricked. After having conversations with people from myriad backgrounds, we are immediately smacked in the face with the reality that only a small percentage of people in the world actually believe what those in our bubble believe. Some of these new people are kind in pointing this out. Others derive great enjoyment from carrying their little pins around and popping people's spiritual bubbles, exposing them to a flood of different and challenging perspectives.

Not everyone's bubble bursts in college, and some bubbles get burst more than others. C. S. Lewis became an atheist after having a staunch, materialist tutor in his late teens but then later reconverted to the faith. Then, after becoming one of the most compelling defenders of God's goodness despite the presence of suffering, his wife died and he questioned whether God was good or really just a pitiless manipulator.[1] Although his bubble was burst many times, C. S. Lewis found his center in God.

More than anything, college is a place of ideas and opinions. We are surrounded by these ideas and opinions from every angle. Professors; new friends from California, New York, the South, the Midwest, or overseas; and even our parents do battle to inform us about what reality is—about what is worth pursuing and how it should be pursued. The unfortunate thing about professors' opinions is (1) we have to listen to them and they know it, and (2) they grade our papers and sometimes make us uneasy about saying things we know they'll disagree with. A few months into our first year, we are most likely knee-deep in disagreeing perspectives about values, beliefs, and theologies with our professors and wonder what is the wise thing to say when writing our term papers.

I can't think of any belief during my four years of college that I didn't put under a microscope and examine. My beliefs about who I am and how I should relate to others were explored. I wanted to know why God created me, what my career should be, and whether or not the right girl was out there waiting for me. I wanted to know exactly who God was, how He administered salvation, whether Christ really rose from the dead, if the Bible was truly inerrant, how homosexuality and abortion should be viewed, and whether there was such a thing as objective right and wrong or whether truth was merely a matter of perspective.

103

TAKING OWNERSHIP OF OUR FAITH

When we begin to explore if what our parents taught us was "true," we begin to take the journey of forming our own identity. This is the essence of the bubble-bursting process. For some it feels like a battle. I know it did for me. I was on a noble quest to find truth, so I read, debated, and questioned as much as I could in hope of finding truth. I knew I was on a search, and those around me knew it as well!

For others, their experiences were much different. They took more passive approaches, so new ideas slowly seeped into their beliefs without their paying much attention to them. Regardless of which path you take, it is important to realize that by the end of college, you will have formed your own beliefs. They will no longer be your parents'; you will be the sole owner.

The incredibly difficult part is when you run across someone who believes the exact opposite as you and has well-thought-out reasons for it. When we meet people who are Mormons or Muslims or whatever with great morals, kind demeanors, and incredible love for others, the idea of God sending them to hell for merely not believing in the right view of Christ may not be as persuasive as it once was. When we find out that less people have even heard of Jesus than who have, it becomes even more difficult to believe God loves everyone equally. When people claim God "seemed" to approve of rape and genocide in the Old Testament, our pictures of God's love and justice can haunt us even more. When our old identity begins to wobble, where will we turn to find our new one?

THE STORY OF TINA

Tina was raised by Christian parents who had high moral and spiritual expectations for her. In response, she got involved in youth ministries, attended church as much as she could, read her Bible daily, and was known among her friends as a spiritual encourager and godly advisor. Then Tina read a book given to her by an atheist for whom she babysat. He argued that we often believe things to be true because of our parents' beliefs, the social environments around us, or an evolutionary desire to survive by creating comforting myths. After deeper conversations with him about his book and finding out his motivation was not one of hating God or Christians but simply of searching for "truth" in Christianity but to no avail, seeds of doubt flooded her mind.

She didn't know what to do. When she remembered how her mother had tearfully reacted when her sister expressed doubts about her faith, Tina felt that within her parents' home, doing so was not an option. In angst, she turned to her spiritual mentor, hoping to share her doubts. But when her mentor heard that she was questioning her spiritual disciplines, instead of asking why (and discerning what the cause might be), Tina's mentor judged and scolded her by saying, "I thought you were stronger than that. I thought you were a real spiritual leader." These comments stung and only made things worse because she wasn't able to find anyone who would listen.

Not knowing where to turn, she prayed to God, but all was silent. Were her childhood beliefs merely a hoax? She prayed again, day after day. Silence. Tina was stuck. She was surrounded by people who expected her to believe something and who didn't provide a caring community in which she could allow herself to be vulnerable. Her spiritual bubble was bursting, and there was no one in sight she could open up to. Sad.

105

ZEAL WITHOUT KNOWLEDGE: LEARNING FROM SOLOMON AND JESUS

Are you passionate about your faith? The Pharisees were. In Tina's story, who was more like the Pharisees? Unfortunately, passion isn't always a good thing. It can be blinding; it can be more easily motivated by pride than by humble searching for the truth. Passion can often disguise and distort. When Jesus healed the blind man, the Pharisees' pride was challenged. God shouldn't allow healings on the Sabbath—they *knew* that. Their bubble was bursting. But instead of trying to discern the cause and effect of why God might allow miracles or trying to see if their values might not be aligned with God's, they instead chose to believe they had it all figured out. They didn't want to see past their own pride and accept that maybe God's truth was beyond theirs. The result was that they commanded the healed man to "give glory to God" by accusing Jesus of being a sinner. When he wouldn't, the Pharisees belittled and condemned the man, who then said, "One thing I do know. I once was blind but now I see!" (John 9:25).

Solomon knew this type of passionate and prideful response well. Thus, he advised, "It is not good to have zeal without knowledge, nor to be hasty and miss the way" (Proverbs 19:2). Instead of taking the time to try and understand people's situations, the Pharisees reacted in anger or spoke quickly for God. With great sadness, I must confess that I have known many people who have treated me as the Pharisees treated the healed man or as the mentor treated Tina, and they were mostly in the church. In fact, all throughout high school, I treated people that same way, but it was before my bubble burst. First Peter 3:15-16 implores us to be able to give a reason for why we believe to anyone who asks, but under one condition: that we do it "with gentleness and respect." When you think of how the church deals with people like Tina, are these the adjectives that come to mind?

In Mark 9:24, a man who wants to see his daughter healed cries out to Jesus, "I do believe; help me overcome my unbelief!" How does Jesus respond? He doesn't yell at the man, belittle him, or condemn him. In fact, He grants his request. Later on, when Thomas can't believe Jesus really is alive after being crucified, does Jesus appear and then condemn? No. He allows Thomas to touch the holes in His hands and His side. He doesn't praise Thomas for his doubts and actually says that those who believe and don't need "proof" are blessed (see John 20:29). But He does show grace and compassion. He does what brings healing because He realizes the value of personally owning one's faith and the consequences of not treating people fairly when they are revaluating their beliefs.

THE POWER AND HEALING OF "I DON'T KNOW"

When I met Tina and talked briefly about some of my doubts, her eyes lit up. She had finally found someone who might understand—and listen. She said that what helped her the most in our discussions was my willingness to say three simple words—"I don't know"—instead of being the "Bible answer man." She called me one day in tears saying how much those words were healing to her. It actually led her to be more open with friends, and soon they all were able to become more vulnerable and experience deeper friendships with each other because of their willingness to express their doubts. God's healing through community was underway.

When I was in high school and college, I thought "I don't know" was like swearing. If I am to be an "ambassador," I must have answers. I devoured commentaries and apologetics books so that I could have the answer—so that I could live out 1 Peter 3:15. The problem was, there weren't always clear answers. The more I strove to push things into black-and-white boxes for every circumstance, the more angry and frustrated I became. Embracing God's mystery seemed like something for the weak of mind, not the "wise." But as I've progressed on my wisdom journey, I've realized the freedom and power of those three words: "I don't know." Don't get me wrong: I am not advocating hiding behind biblical verses like "God's ways are beyond our ways" (see Isaiah 55:8-9) as an intellectual crutch when I start seeing inconsistencies in my logic. Rather,

I had to come to grips with the fact that in some areas, there are a couple different ways of looking at things and I honestly didn't know which way was right.

THE LAUNDRY LIST OF BUBBLE-BURSTING WISDOM

So how do you maintain the practices of faith that will sustain you and help you grow in the chaos of having everything in your life challenged?

Pursue Humility

Humility is really important in responding wisely in the bubble-bursting process. Will you be humble when your bubble starts to burst? When you have doubts, will you seek guidance from friends and mentors who have walked the journey longer than you, or can you figure it all out on your own? Will your words heal, or will they tear down? Will you have the courage in conversations to admit sometimes that you just don't know?

Learn from Solomon

Proverbs 15 and 16 so powerfully address the issues I've been discussing that they don't need an explanation. Read slowly, soak them in, and think about how they apply to a person whose bubble is bursting.

> *A gentle answer turns away wrath, but a harsh word stirs up anger. (Proverbs 15:1)*

> *The tongue that brings healing is a tree of life. (Proverbs 15:4)*

The heart of the righteous weighs its answers, but the mouth of the wicked gushes evil. (Proverbs 15:28)

The fear of the LORD teaches a man wisdom, and humility comes before honor. (Proverbs 15:33)

The LORD tears down the proud man's house. (Proverbs 15:25)

All a man's ways seem innocent to him, but motives are weighed by the LORD. (Proverbs 16:2)

The LORD detests all the proud of heart. (Proverbs 16:5)

Pride goes before destruction, a haughty spirit before a fall. Better to be lowly in spirit. (Proverbs 16:18-19)

The wise in heart are called discerning, and pleasant words promote instruction. (Proverbs 16:21)

109

A wise man's heart guides his mouth, and his lips promote instruction. (Proverbs 16:23)

Pleasant words are a honeycomb, sweet to the soul and healing to the bones. (Proverbs 16:24)

Better a patient man than a warrior. (Proverbs 16:32)

There is a way that seems right to a man, but in the end it leads to death. (Proverbs 16:25)

Explore but Stay Connected

If Jesus could articulate the beliefs of the Pharisees and Sadducees, and if Paul could articulate most of the Greek philosophies, then it makes sense that our goal as Christians is not to insulate our thinking. In fact, once we hit the college scene, it's impossible to do so. As we pursue friendships, it is okay to be available and open to new ideas without being angry and emotionally defensive. Developing an understanding of other people's worlds so that you know where they are coming from is *not* the same as embracing their beliefs. However, it is vital that during this process you find a few resources to stay connected. Solomon urges, "Guard your heart, for it is the wellspring of life" (Proverbs 4:23).

First, identify some core friends and mentors you respect who regularly practice wisdom—people constantly trying to stay aligned with God's perspective on life, people who realize alignment involves GPS-like points of reference to the questions *Am I doing the right (just) thing? Am I valuing the right thing? Can I discern the consequences?* Plan time to be with those people regularly. Make sure they are the kind of people you can "air your dirty laundry of doubts" to without feeling condemned or criticized.

110

Get Connected to a Local Church

Let's face it: if your average bedtime in college is 2 AM, getting up early enough to go to church can be difficult. And depending on what activities you engaged in on Saturday night, you might not be excited to hear messages about holiness. However, there are a variety of reasons that getting connected to a church is a good idea. Most of the reasons center around the fact that doing so helps you consider and practice how to stay aligned with God's viewpoints.

By connected, I don't mean sampling every church in the area for four years to see which ones have the cutest girls or guys. Nor am I saying going to a variety of churches from different denominations is a bad idea. It's not. Doing so can help you expand your bubble to understand others' points of view and be able to relate to them better. However, chronic church-hopping isn't exactly the same as finding spiritual roots.

SURVIVING THE BURST WISELY

During the arduous process of bursting or expanding their spiritual bubbles, wise people acknowledge their need for others and their need for God despite no longer being confident of what they truly know about God.

THINK ABOUT IT

1. What makes up your "bubble" and how do you think it affects the way you live your life—relationships with God and others, school, job?

111

2. How does God want to use the bubble-bursting process in your life or in someone else's you might know?

3. What did you learn from this chapter that could apply to your life?

SPEED DIAL:
HOW TO PICK MY FRIENDS WHEN SPACE IS LIMITED

I love to climb mountains. I love getting up early at camp (well, not too early) with great friends, getting our packs ready, and heading up the trail. Each day has its own challenges (a sudden storm might blow in) and rewards (we might see a distant mountain range we've never seen before). By afternoon our muscles hurt from the climb, and our sides ache from laughing so much. There's one factor, though, that makes these climbs richer and more rewarding than anything else. It's not the particular mountain we're climbing, and it's not the time of year. It's not the kind of food we've packed, and it's not how grueling or easy the climb turns out to be. It's the choice of friends who make the climb. Experiencing life with them makes the trip valuable.

I've heard it said that the quality of our lives is determined by our friendships—not by how much money we make, what kind of car we drive, how many awards we receive, or even our family background. Poet and statesman Joseph Addison stated, "The greatest sweetener of human life is friendship."[1] And the English philosopher Francis Bacon observed the impact of genuine friendship on us: "It redoubles joy and cuts grief in half."[2] Isn't that the truth? When something is fun, it is much more fun when we enjoy it with someone else. And when we are down, our sorrow is comforted by someone who understands and cares.

Novelist Ethel Watts Mumford once observed, "God gives us our relatives—thank God we can choose our friends."[3] But friends require a choice. Like the number of speed-dial slots on our phones, the space in our lives to maintain meaningful friendships is limited.

The ability to choose the right friends is one of the most important skills we will ever acquire in our lives. I honestly believe this may be the most important chapter in section 2 of this book. Friends validate who we are, what we do, and what we value.

PICKING FRIENDS IN COLLEGE – DO YOU CARE ABOUT THE SAME TRUTH?

Some of us grew up in the same house all through our precollege years and had the same friends from elementary school through high school graduation. Our circle of friends was limited to the geography of our neighborhoods and towns. We went to class together, played sports together, and socialized together. But when we walk onto the college campus, we have new ways of picking friends. Now geography means far less. Yes, we may become friends with people who live in our dorm, apartment, or Greek house, but we rub shoulders every day with people from all over the country—and all over the world. Our interests—rather than geography—often direct our choices of friends.

In his excellent book *The Four Loves*,[4] C. S. Lewis points out that common interests are the backbone of friendship. He says, "A typical expression of opening Friendship would be something like 'What? You too? I thought I was the only one.'" Lewis further notes Ralph Waldo Emerson's insight that when a friend thinks or asks, "Do you love me?" he really means, "Do you see the same truth?"—or at least, "Do you *care about* the same truth?" In essence,

Lewis is saying that we choose our friends because we agree with what they *value*. Those whose purpose is to party will often choose friends who will stay out all night with them. Those who are driven to excel academically often gravitate to those who value learning and high grades. And those who want to follow Christ look for relationships that encourage each other to make great decisions that honor the Lord. A wise freshman chooses friends based on their values and often asks, "Are their pursuits worthwhile? Do they care about the consequences of their actions? Are our common interests morally right?"

EARLY EXPERIENCES: ROOMMATES AND THE ORIENTATION WHIRLWIND

People who we typically have no choice about rubbing shoulders with are our roommates. For at least the first semester, we are stuck with who we get. Sharing a room with someone you don't know very well can be a very challenging experience, especially if you have little in common. Some people have great expectations of becoming best friends with their roommates. But what will you do when you hoped you'd become good friends with your roommate but now can't stand anything he or she does? How will you find the time to discern the cause and effect of your irritations? What steps will you take to ensure that your words are "seasoned with the salt of grace" instead of lashing out in hurtful ways when you are stressed out by school deadlines, all-nighters, and a lack of sleep? Although difficult, it is best to avoid responding to conflict passive-aggressively or with sarcasm.

The roommate experience can often be one of the best but most difficult training grounds for developing the key friend-ship skills of forgiveness, honesty, gentleness, grace, and open

115

communication. The wise take the time to consider what God wants them to learn through the roommate journey. The answers don't usually come after five minutes of prayer for God to "fix" your roommate.

To some degree, our major of study plays a key role in who we choose as friends (although I've known people who changed majors so often that they knew every person on campus). In the fluid dynamics of the college campus, our circle of friends can change quickly. With the flurry of orientation activities designed to help the friend-making process and the freedom to hang out with these new people anytime you want because you aren't restricted to a parental curfew, opportunities abound. What will you value in looking for a friend? How will you react when a friend you were forming a strong bond with suddenly seems more interested in hanging out with other people? The truth is, the freshman year is one of the biggest times of change in people's lives.

THE WAY JESUS CHOSE HIS FRIENDS

Think about how Jesus chose His friends. Before reading further, take a few moments to jot down a few ways He did this. Seriously. What can we learn from Jesus' actions? If His life was the essence of Proverbs in living color, there should be much to learn from Him. He selected His closest friends by spending all night in prayer. From that group of friends, He developed an inner circle consisting of Peter, James, and John, who were with Him at the most sacred of events, such as the Transfiguration. He entrusted one of His inner-circle friends with taking care of His mother after His death on the cross.

What did He look for in a friend? Did He look for perfect people? No. In fact, He even chose people who abandoned Him at

His greatest time of need, but that didn't stop Him from forgiving them for their failure and entrusting them with the incredible responsibility of the Great Commission. Jesus took the time to see to the core of each person, not judging the outward appearance but seeing the true worth of "average" fishermen and despised tax collectors. He defined true friendship when He said, "Greater love has no one than this, that he lay down his life for his friends" (John 15:13).

It's powerful to remember that Jesus lived what He preached. Jesus chose His inner circle wisely but didn't restrict His interactions to only them. He stretched His comfort zone and spent time with lots of different kinds of people (poor, unpopular, rich, superreligious), even those who misunderstood and frustrated Him the most.

Jesus said we are to be *in* the world but not *of* the world (see John 17:14-18). That means we are to relate in meaningful ways with people of all stripes, sizes, and colors. We don't have to believe what they believe, and we don't have to do what they do. But a mature, wise person can be a friend to almost anybody. I know a young woman who is a resident assistant. On her floor are lesbians, bisexuals, and girls with very different values. She is a strong Christian, but she developed good friendships with all the girls on her floor. She truly strives to live as Jesus did.

As we spend time with people who don't share our values, it's important to remember the difference between liking them and being like them. Jesus spent lots of time with tax gatherers, but He didn't become one. He also spent time with people who partied hard, but He didn't get drunk with them. Instead, Jesus changed the lives of any and all who were open to His love and truth. Wise people realize they don't have the powers Jesus did at abstaining from sin. Taking time to reflect on how our friends are influencing us, despite how good our intentions are to be a good influence on them, is time well invested. An inner circle of trusted friends who point out our blind spots can be pivotal in showing us what God's values for right relationships might be.

THE MEANING OF A TRUE FRIEND

A true friend is loyal.

There have been a few people who I could trust completely not to breathe a word of anything I wanted kept in confidence. Loyalty is one of the chief characteristics of friendship, and it goes way beyond keeping your mouth shut. A true friend "sticks closer than a brother" (Proverbs 18:24). He or she is committed to you no matter what. Even if you are doubting your faith to the highest degree in an attempt to sort out what you truly believe, a friend will support you. Even if (and when) you do something completely stupid, intentionally or unintentionally, a friend will stand by you. In Ecclesiastes 4:10, Solomon says,

118

> *If one falls down,*
> *his friend can help him up.*
> *But pity the man who falls*
> *and has no one to help him up!*

We need friends who can help us in tough times, be there for us, and stick closer than a brother.

First Samuel describes one of the most beautiful stories in the Bible: the friendship between David and Jonathan, King Saul's son. David had killed Goliath and saved the nation, but Saul was jealous over David's popularity. He wanted to have the young warrior killed. Jonathan risked his own life, time and again, to defend David, and supported his friend when no one else in the kingdom was willing to help David. In one of the best classic descriptions of true friendship in all of literature, the Bible says, "The soul of Jonathan was knit to the soul of David" (1 Samuel 18:1, NASB). These men truly loved each other and were prepared to die for each other. That kind of loyalty is sometimes stated but seldom real. Jonathan and David had the real thing.

A true friend is honest.

Solomon wrote, "An honest answer is like a kiss on the lips" (Proverbs 24:26). One of the tests of friendship is whether people are willing to speak the truth to each other and risk a negative reaction. Solomon also wrote, "Wounds from a friend can be trusted, but an enemy multiplies kisses" (Proverbs 27:6). There have been times when close friends, such as my wife, had the courage to say, "Mark, **119** I really care about you, and I need to tell you something." At that point, I know the bomb bay doors are opening and the bomb is about to drop. Then I have the choice to either value my friend's courage and honesty or hunker down in my emotional bomb shelter and hope the truth goes away. Although brutal honesty is usually hard to hear, I've learned to value it even more than much of the encouragement I get.

Great friendships work "as iron sharpens iron" (Proverbs 27:17). For example, many during college will choose to go out clubbing Saturday nights because dancing with the opposite sex makes them feel more attractive and accepted. This excitement is often bittersweet and short-lived yet often feels more "real" and "tangible" than Sunday-morning church. Sometimes the aftermath ends in skipping church the next morning because of feeling too tired or guilty. Real friends help their friends realize that what they're really looking for can't be captured by the clubbing experience. They see why wisdom isn't sexy but is so valuable.

A true friend is forgiving.

In any real friendship, people's feelings are going to be hurt. Many years ago, a leading character in the movie *Love Story* said, "Love means never having to say you're sorry." After careful analysis and deep reflection, I'd have to say, "That's bunk." Love means being willing to say that you're sorry, and it means forgiving those who hurt us. Sometimes we need to excuse somebody's bad day. We need to give people some space to get over whatever is bothering them. Paul wrote to the believers in Colossae, "Bear with each other and forgive whatever grievances you may have against one another. Forgive as the Lord forgave you" (Colossians 3:13). Forgiveness means we acknowledge how hurt we are but choose to not hold the offense against that person.

True friends are good forgivers. They overlook it after we've ditched them to hang out with our new dating interest, but they're honest enough to tell us we hurt them. They discern that the angry words we spoke were really displaced on them from another source, possibly from the pressure our parents are putting on us to live up to their expectations. They discern with patience, they help us use our failures as tools to learn, and they help us forgive ourselves and others. In short, they make good use of the points of reference and speed bumps to help us mend our lives by realigning with God's perspective. But they do it with tact and with our interests in mind, not just theirs.

A true friend is realistic.

Friends don't sign up to be our parents or our teachers, or to fill the role of God in our lives. Don't expect them to do more than be a friend. When we expect (or demand) more than friendship, we put a tremendous strain on the relationship. In college, a friend of mine developed relationships with a lot of girls, and he was really drawn to one girl in particular. She was really kind and sweet. He pursued her and tried to spend as much time with her as possible, but soon I noticed something was wrong. The more he pursued, the more she backed away. I knew this guy was from a difficult background. His parents were divorced, and his dad was an alcoholic. I think he was looking for more than friendship. He was hoping this girl would fill the hole in his heart left by his family's hurts. Before long, the girl backed away completely, leaving him devastated. What this guy needed was a friend who would help him discern the deeper realities of the situation, treat him with grace and love, and show him how much God values him.

121

Another thing I've noticed about the reality of friendships is that they sometimes end. Someone moves away. Someone changes values and lifestyle. Someone gets in with a different crowd. Many times, we can stay friends even at a distance, but it's just not the same as seeing the person regularly and sharing dreams and dreads on a daily basis. It hurts when two friends are separated or when we change and move on.

WHAT ELSE TO LOOK FOR

To see if someone has the qualities of a true friend, look for words, actions, reactions, and direction. These are often the more obvious clues to uncovering the more subtle qualities of loyalty, honesty, forgiveness, and realism.

Words. Listen to what people talk about. Do they talk at all about seeking God and His kingdom, or are they obsessed with pleasure, approval, power, status, and things? Does their humor destroy or build up people? I can't tell you how many times I've caught myself repeating a phrase or joke I heard from another friend. Listen closely to discern if you want to be seen as talking like those you hang around with.

Actions. Some people say the right things but don't back up their words through their actions. This can be especially true at Christian universities. A person's behavior tells more about his values and convictions than his verbiage does, so take notice of what people do, where they go, and how they handle responsibilities. Those things tell you how much, and in what areas, you can trust someone.

Reactions. Watch for people's reactions to success and failure, to joys and disappointments. If a person gets angry quickly and at small problems, steer clear. On the other hand, you'll see wisdom in those who pray for needs, care about others' hurts, listen well, and stand strong on their convictions.

Direction. Each person is going forward, backward, or standing still. Most college students change their minds a time or two about their careers, but the wise ones always plan their lives around the direction God gives them.

THE ART OF BEING ALONE

To be the best friend you can be, take time to be alone. I've already written about the importance of reflection and the need to carve out time to think about each day's events. People who don't reflect often make impulsive decisions, and impulsive choices often lead to heartache. Jesus loved people like no one else ever has or ever will, but He made sure He spent time alone to think, pray, and recharge His emotional and spiritual batteries. If Christ—God in the flesh who had all knowledge and wisdom—needed to get away from people regularly to get a fresh perspective, I need it far more!

Sometimes our time alone is not really our choice. Some students have a difficult time finding a place to fit in. They feel lonely, especially when they see so many people around them having a great time together. This isn't the time to make a snap decision to jump into a group. The Lord is preparing you and a group of people for wonderful friendships. Pray, think, and be ready when that time comes. But don't be passive. Take steps toward people. Get to know them, ask questions, and listen carefully. Some of us are very hesitant to develop new friendships because we've been burned before. That's completely understandable, but don't let past hurts keep you from building new friendships. Learn from the past, but don't let it master you. Forgive yourself, forgive those who hurt you, and be wise so you don't put too much trust in untrustworthy people again. Most of all, be open to the Lord's leading to new friendships. Ask Him to help you discern how your friends are influencing you, where He is using others to speak truth into your life, and where He might want you to support a friend in need through word or deed.

THINK ABOUT IT

1. Who are your friends right now and how do you think they affect you? Positively? Negatively? Explain.

2. Why do you think it's important to choose your friends wisely? How can you practically do that?

3. How does God want to use friendships in your life? How has He used them in the past?

4. What did you learn from this chapter that could apply to your life?

TIME IS MONEY:
IS TIME REALLY THE MOST IMPORTANT RESOURCE?

In high school, everything is planned out for us. We start school at a certain time, we have lunch at a certain time, and we end school at a certain time. If we spend our time ditching class, a school administrator will probably call our parents informing them of our truancy. In short, there is a built-in system to help us succeed in time management, academically at least.

In college it's quite different. We're free. We choose which classes we take, and usually they aren't every day from eight till two. We can have four hours between classes that tempt us to make a run to the beach with our new friends or go to the mall to get those new shoes we saw someone wearing. Some days, we might not have class at all. Because everyone has different schedules for breaks or lunch, we have to plan when we want to go to the cafeteria and eat with our friends. And that's just during the day. Without curfew and with the incredible number of people we want to meet and make mischief with, we often times don't go to bed before 2 AM. Getting up by seven to get to class on time and find the right parking spot at our high school is long gone. All we have to do is roll out of bed and walk a few hundred yards to class.

After two months in school, it's quite common for freshmen to realize there is great difficulty in balancing time. The competing demands of an exciting new social life with no curfew, working out enough to feel like we are looking good, not getting too far behind early on in the semester, and finding time for God and family or the long-distance girlfriend or boyfriend can be overwhelming. Before we know it, we are two chapters behind in reading for all our classes, and midterms are next week.

A SOPHOMORE AFTER FOUR YEARS?

Let a story about the lives of some of my friends illustrate the severity. Three of my friends all went to the same college right out of high school. They always ate lunch off campus and usually skipped their afternoon classes for more interesting activities. Homework and grades were worthless to them. They became stuck in a cycle of starting off well in the first week of the semester, then slacking off from there on out, and needing to drop half their classes so they wouldn't fail. Four years later, they were still sophomores, and at about the time they wanted to start settling down to get married, they realized they had no savings (but pretty big credit card debt), no job, no ability to provide, but finally some much-needed ambition. Like Solomon looking back on his life of pleasure seeking and feeling that it was chasing after the wind, so too these guys now look at their first four years of college with regret that they didn't spend their time more wisely. Thankfully, my friends hit some crucial speed bumps in their lives that steered them to the right path. They have mustered up the courage to learn from their failures, forgive themselves, and look to God for strength and wisdom as they continue their journeys.

TIME AS MONEY

Some have said that time is our most valuable commodity. In the movie *The Family Man*, we see Nicholas Cage's character struggling over the value of time as money. In the movie, he is a disgustingly rich, ambitious, unmarried banker. On Christmas Eve, he falls asleep and dreams about what his life would have been like had he been a tire salesman and decided to get married instead of pursue his career. He sees that his family wouldn't have been able to afford even one of the suits he wears every day as a banker but that his life ultimately would have been much richer and more valuable if he had aligned his priorities to value others more than himself. Although the movie doesn't have God as a major theme, it clearly depicts that having the right values can make the difference in how fulfilling our time will be.

As my friends look back at their wasted "investments," they agree completely. In fact, when they heard I was writing this book, they said I had to title this chapter "Time Is Money" because that's what it truly was for them. A quick calculation of their current just-above-minimum-wage jobs compared to what they would be making had they already graduated is woeful. Although many people reading this book will probably be sophomores after their first year of college, how wisely they will have spent their time may still be an issue. As many of us know, having good grades isn't the only important pursuit in college. But what is? Friends, family, God? Many of us might quickly say yes to that list, but if we take the time to write out where we actually spend our time, will our actions match our words?

THE PRIORITIES TEST — HOW MUCH WORTH DOES GOD ASCRIBE TO THIS?

If anyone would have told me when I was in college that God wasn't the most important thing in my life, I'd have said they just didn't know me. But one day, I began to analyze just how much time I actually spent cultivating my faith. Let's see: every movie I watch is two hours, and I watch at least two or three with friends a week. That's good. It's time spent with friends, but is it quality time where I'm actually developing a deeper, more meaningful friendship? Do I spend time with God for even 25 percent of the time I allot for movies? If I'm honest, no. In fact, when I added up time spent with God, family, and my closest friends back home, it still wasn't half of the time I spent merely watching movies or playing video games with my dorm mates. Now, those experiences aren't in themselves bad things, but put into proper perspective, they surely aren't more valuable than those who have helped shape me at my core.

Before reading on, do a simple exercise: Estimate quickly how much time per week you spend (1) watching movies, (2) listening to music, (3) working out or "laying out," (4) shopping, and (5) getting ready so that you "look good" before going out. Now compare that with time spent (1) praying or trying to connect with God in some way, (2) catching up with close friends on the phone or in person, and (3) letting your family know how things are going in your life. Is it comparable? Jesus says where our treasure is, there our hearts will be also (see Matthew 6:21). If time is a treasure, where do we add up?

SOLOMON AND JESUS ON TIME MANAGEMENT

In the later years of his life Solomon was not the greatest example of time well spent, but early on he had his priorities right. He wrote down some tips about the wisdom of discipline and diligence and how these two traits can severely impact the quality of our lives. "The sluggard craves and gets nothing, but the desires of the diligent are fully satisfied" (Proverbs 13:4). He also said wise people learn from even the menial things in their surroundings:

Go to the ant, you sluggard;
consider its ways and be wise!
It has no commander,
no overseer or ruler,
yet it stores its provisions in summer
and gathers its food at harvest.

How long will you lie there, you sluggard?
When will you get up from your sleep?
A little sleep, a little slumber,
a little folding of the hands to rest—
and poverty will come on you like a bandit
and scarcity like an armed man. (Proverbs 6:6-11)

Wow, that sounds just like my friends. No overseer of their schedule, a little sleep, a little slacking, poverty striking, their need great. The parallel is powerful. Unfortunately, Solomon wasn't very consistent in the area of priorities. By his middle years, the sheer number of wives and concubines he amassed (nearly one thousand) was enough to take up all his time. His life alarmingly illustrates that even the wisest man on earth can be taken down with just a few decisions out of alignment with God's values.

In contrast to Solomon's up-and-down ride with time management, Jesus was a much more consistent and positive example. He spent much of His time doing things that really mattered, such as healing people and caring for the oppressed and outcast—for example, those who we sometimes don't make time to talk to because we are too busy. (See Luke 10:30-37, the Good Samaritan story, for further reflection.) Yet He also made time to celebrate and socialize with friends. His first miracle was turning water to wine at a wedding celebration. Furthermore, after long and draining days of miraculous works, He often woke up "very early in the morning, while it was still dark . . . and went off to a solitary place, where he prayed" (Mark 1:35). But Jesus also showed incredible insight and balance for those who err on overproducing. When Martha was stressing to get all she deemed important done, she pleaded for Jesus to command Mary to help her. Jesus replied gently, "Martha, Martha, you are worried and bothered about so many things; but only one thing is necessary, for Mary has chosen the good part" (Luke 10:41-42, NASB). Did you get that? Only one thing is needed. What is that one thing in your life? Does it include things that benefit yourself or others? Does it build up your physique or your spiritual life?

MAKING THE MOST OF EVERY OPPORTUNITY

If we look at the people or history around us, we can see those who really treasure making good use of their time, and others who don't. ATMs and fast-food have given us more time, but how do we use it? Consider the apostle Paul, who was tortured, hands and feet in stocks, but who chose "singing hymns of praise to God" to fill his time (Acts 16:25, NASB). Later on, when his hands were free, he penned Ephesians, Philippians, Colossians, and Philemon. He clearly practiced what he preached, as in these letters, he urges us to "be very careful, then, how you live—not as unwise but as wise, making the most of every opportunity, because the days are evil" (Ephesians 5:15-16) and "whatever you do, work at it with all your heart, as working for the Lord, not for men" (Colossians 3:23).

One of my roommates slept about thirteen hours a night, whereas another had a "system" of sleeping three hours a night and taking several short naps throughout the day. These are two drastically different approaches to making the most of the day. Admittedly, some seem to go overboard—such as Einstein wearing the same clothes every day to save time and mental energy, or the founder of organizational psychology reading a book while plowing in the cornfields—but their efforts are worth considering. They truly made the most of every opportunity.

When I discovered how much time I spent reading comics and watching movies, I decided I needed to make a change. It wasn't easy, but I decided that every day I didn't spend time in devotionals with God, I wouldn't lift weights or run—things I had been doing six days a week. At first this resulted in neither working out nor spending time with God, but I stayed true to my promise. Over time I began a habit of journaling out my prayers in the morning so that my mind wouldn't wander. Later on I realized that when I was too tired from studying, I could take prayer walks to get some fresh air, clear my mind, and try to make God a part of my life instead of turning on the TV to veg.

Finally, and maybe most important, I decided I wanted to have more meaningful conversations with the new people I was meeting. Instead of the usual questions everyone asks (What's your major? Where are you from? Why did you choose this school?), I decided to create more meaningful questions to ask. With help from a friend, I created five new questions:

1. What are a few of your strengths, characteristics, or accomplishments that you are most proud of?

2. What are a few of your weaknesses?

3. What are a few of your fears and insecurities?

4. What is something you regret or something you learned a valuable lesson from?

5. What are your dreams or passions in life?

Although these questions weren't used with everyone (so people wouldn't think I was too weird), when they were used, they opened the door for the Holy Spirit to work in developing conversations and friendships that truly mattered in my life. In a few months, the things I had learned from others through using my time differently were astounding. Further, my friendships felt much more enriching. After setting some clear priorities for my life, bouncing them off my close friends and mentor, and doing the hard work of finding the time to actually live them out, I began to see spiritual and social growth that was unparalleled in my life. The time invested was well worth it.

The truth is, everyone has twenty-four "hour dollars" to spend in a day. What we do with them is what counts. Will we take the time to consider how our priorities are affecting our personal life and our relationships with those around us? Will we discern the cause-and-effect difference between watching a movie with a friend versus having a conversation over coffee about something meaningful? Most likely we will pause long enough to wonder what God's values are for our big decisions, but what about for our routine activities? In only three years, Jesus changed the shape and even the dating system (BC/AD) of the world. For Jesus, a steady diet of just living included serving others' needs, witnessing about God's kingdom, spending time with close friends, celebrating, praying, and experiencing solitude. That was how Jesus chose to spend His time. How will you?

THINK ABOUT IT

1. What consumes most of your time? Is this a good thing, or do you feel your life is out of balance?

2. How do you think your current schedule affects you and your relationships with God and others?

3. How does God want to use time management in your life? How has He used it in the past?

4. What did you learn from this chapter that could apply to your life?

HOOKUP OR HANG-UP?
WISDOM AND OPPOSITE-SEX ENCOUNTERS

Let's all be honest with ourselves: college is a major opportunity to hang out with members of the opposite sex, and hookup opportunities abound. God is all for having sex—after all, He created genders and the entire concept of marriage. But if we aren't careful, our desire to "hook up" can become a hang-up. It's a good idea to remember that the purpose of meeting those of the opposite sex is not to have an emotional partner, love interest, or good time; you should be preparing for marriage. So you want to have the right perspective on what you are searching for; you want to be aligned with God's values and God's morality and have an understanding of how your actions will affect you and others. Let's see how proper alignment can apply to relationships.

LEARNING FROM MISTAKES

I came to college with a very simple idea of how my life in college would work out: I would fall in love with the girl of my dreams somewhere around my junior year, we would get engaged my senior year, and we'd get married shortly after graduation. It was not my ultimate goal of attending college, but it was definitely in the back of my mind.

A friend of mine, we'll call him Steve, came to college with a different plan: he already had a girlfriend, and they would get married in his sophomore or junior year when she entered college. Even though upperclassmen told him they would eventually break up, he insisted their relationship was the real deal.

Then there were the girls who pursued "MRS" degrees. Their objective was to marry Mr. Right and become Mrs. Right and then drop out and raise families (an admirable life objective for some, but we still made fun of them).

When we all left school in 1991, I had no fiancée, Steve had broken up with his high school sweetheart and married someone else, and the girls looking for their "MRS" degrees were glad they had majored in something else, because they were going to need jobs until Mr. Right came along and swept them off their feet.

Of all the do-overs I'd like to be granted, most of them involve the way I handled myself in relationships with the opposite sex. I was just not wise enough (my girlfriends might have used the phrase "mature enough") to enter into the kind of intense relationships that college offers. Relationships for me became real hang-ups.

FINDING "THE ONE"

Before college, I went to a "computer dance." Basically we filled out surveys and fed them into a computer, which then predicted our best match. When you arrived at the dance, you received a numbered name tag and were supposed to find the person with the matching number and at least have one dance with him or her. I searched the room and eventually found the one the computer had chosen for me: the school librarian.

While I didn't like the results of my computer experience, I liked how easy it was to find "the one." What if God just gave us all numbers at birth and we found His best match for us simply by matching numbers? Wouldn't that be easy? While God hasn't revealed "exact matches" for us, He does give us principles to search with. But before we discuss them, let's ask an important question: *Why is the pursuit of "the one" so important to us?*

One simple answer to this question is that movies and advertisements hype up our desire for romantic love. Another answer could be that our Sunday school teachers might have told us that God has made one special person for us (never mind that statistically this is impossible because there are more women than men in the world). Knowing this can be reassuring for some but stressful for those of us who feel pressured to make sure we find our soul mates. The movie *Jerry Maguire* illustrates both of these possible answers to why we feel we must pursue "the one." After a tumultuous ride in a relationship he rushed into too quickly because he "hates being alone," Jerry rushes to her house after an exciting moment of realizing "she is the one." As he dashes into her living room, he passionately exclaims the phrase we all secretly want to hear: "You complete me."

137

This belief that there's someone out there who can "complete" us clearly motivates many of our actions. But is it true? First of all, even the term "the one" suggests some all-sufficient person who will be able to take care of our every need, understand and treat us perfectly, and have passionate romantic encounters with us for the rest of our lives. Is this realistic? Of course not, so we must realize that the term doesn't mean all-sufficient but rather the one who we will be very, if not most, compatible with to enjoy a meaningful marriage. Second, what is behind this desire for the person who completes us? Larry Crabb suggests in a variety of his books, especially in *Understanding People,*[1] that there are two basic motivations that drive us: finding significance and finding security. Significance can include a desire for impact, achievement, and appreciation for something we have done. Security can include a desire for deep relationship that makes us feel safe, protected, cherished, and loved. The former, Crabb says, is more common for males and the latter for females, although both genders can be motivated by either.

When I look at my own life, I notice that I like to feel I've accomplished something significant and that my actions have great *value*—that they have had a meaningful impact. Crabb believes that these cravings can find their fulfillment only in God.[2] Although I'm not certain we find fulfillment for these cravings only in God, I think He is definitely the only "one source" of them for "in him we live and move and have our being" (Acts 17:28). Or as David pleads after realizing his great sin in seeing Bathsheba and being willing to do anything in his power to have her,

Create in me a pure [new] heart, O God. . . .
Restore to me the joy of your salvation
    and grant me a willing spirit, to sustain me.
    (Psalm 51:10, 12)*

The degree to which we or others are aligned with realizing that one person can't complete us (cause and effect) and that God is the true source of our joy (values), the more I feel we are able to find true fulfillment from God and from others in the right way (justice). What do you think?

VALUING THE RIGHT THINGS IN A MARRIAGE PARTNER

Ultimately, whether we believe in the concept of "the one" or not isn't as important as whether we look for the right characteristics in a marriage partner. The right traits can be a little different for girls than they are for guys, so we'll detail them separately.

LADIES, FIND A MAN WHO . . .

Seeks After God

> A man's steps are directed by the LORD.
>> How then can anyone understand his own way?
>> (Proverbs 20:24)
>
> There is no wisdom, no insight, no plan
>> that can succeed against the LORD. (Proverbs 21:30)

I must admit there is a shortage of guys who seek after God during the college years. It takes us guys a little longer to realize our need to depend completely on God, especially if we are driven by a desire for significance and achievement. While a man who loves God may be hard to come by, wait until you find him. Without God your guy will be lost, and he'll probably take you with him.

Shows Leadership Qualities

> Wives, submit to your husbands as to the Lord. For the husband is the head of the wife as Christ is the head of the church, his body, of which he is the Savior. Now as the church submits to Christ, so also wives should submit to their husbands in everything.
>> Husbands, love your wives, just as Christ loved the church and gave himself up for her. (Ephesians 5:22-25)

God's design for families is for husbands to be in leadership; note that does not mean "lordship." You want to find a guy who knows where he is going in life and who you are willing to submit to. I have found very few women who have difficulty with this idea if they are in a relationship with a man who truly loves them like Christ loves the church, so look for this quality. Leadership does not mean he has to be a public speaker or hold an office; it just means he is going someplace you are willing to go too.

Is Kind

A kind man benefits himself,
but a cruel man brings trouble on himself. (Proverbs 11:17)

I know so many girls with low self-esteem who let guys just trash them up because they feel a decent guy could never love them. I also know girls who just have a thing for guys in trouble. They are inveterate "fixers" yet don't realize that only God can truly do the fixing. Proverbs shows us the effects of kindness and trouble. If you want to benefit your life, find a kind man; otherwise you may find yourself living out an episode of Jerry Springer.

GUYS, FIND A WOMAN WHO . . .

Seeks After God

But seek first his kingdom and his righteousness, and all these
things will be given to you as well. (Matthew 6:33)

There is nothing more beautiful than a woman who loves God with her whole self. You should be seeking God, and likewise you want a woman in your life who is doing the same. Let me give you a tip, guys: the right girl is seeking God and looking for a guy who also is, so figure it out.

Possesses a Good Character

Solomon's wives did him in. Perhaps that is why he repeatedly addresses this issue in the proverbs he collected. Just look at what he has to say:

> *A wife of noble character is her husband's crown,*
>   *but a disgraceful wife is like decay in his bones.*
>   *(Proverbs 12:4)*

> *Better to live on a corner of the roof*
>   *than share a house with a quarrelsome wife.*
>   *(Proverbs 21:9)*

> *A wife of noble character who can find?*
>   *She is worth far more than rubies. (Proverbs 31:10)*

141

Clearly, the woman you want is one who has a noble character. A great indicator of a female with this quality is to what extent she exudes the fruit of the Spirit. Do you *and* others (I say others because it's easy to have our thinking cloud when romantic feelings flare) see her as having "love, joy, peace, patience, kindness, goodness, faithfulness, gentleness and self-control" (Galatians 5:22)? Now think about how she strives to live these characteristics out with friends, with her roommate, with her mom and dad, and at church. Of course, no one is perfect, but is she at least striving? One of my concerns about marriage was if I would be able to remain faithful to one person all my life. While that is ultimately a matter of my personal integrity, having found a woman I can treasure makes it that much less a concern.

Possesses Inner Beauty

Our culture in the United States focuses far too much on outward beauty. In fact, it is very difficult for many guys to be able to appreciate or even see the inner beauty of most women because we have been so exposed to the flesh. One of the greatest threats to our ability to see what really makes a woman beautiful is pornography. If you want to see a woman for who God made her to be, you have to focus on the inner self. Consider Peter's letter to the church:

> *Your beauty should not come from outward adornment, such as braided hair and the wearing of gold jewelry and fine clothes. Instead, it should be that of your inner self, the unfading beauty of a gentle and quiet spirit, which is of great worth in God's sight. For this is the way the holy women of the past who put their hope in God used to make themselves beautiful.* (1 Peter 3:3-5)

Did you catch that? Unfading beauty. My wife is beautiful on the outside, but what if she became horribly disfigured? (She just loves my what-ifs.) Would I leave her? Absolutely not, because I fell in love with her inner beauty, and that will not fade. I had a teacher once who had been badly scarred in an auto accident. I must admit that when I first saw her, I did not think she was attractive at all. By the end of the semester, I had a much different impression. Her inner beauty was so great that it overshadowed her scars, and I found her to be quite attractive. It may take time, but look intently for this quality.

VALUING YOUR SEXUAL IDENTITY

When it comes to sexual activity, the world's wisdom and God's wisdom could not be further from each other. Sex is a wonderful creation. God designed it, made it, and knew we would love Him for it. In fact, according to Genesis 1:28, He commanded Adam and Eve to be fruitful and multiply (there is only one way to do that).

But God did not design sex for just the function of procreation; He actually encourages us to enjoy it. Take a look at what is written in Proverbs:

> *May your fountain be blessed,*
>> *and may you rejoice in the wife of your youth.*
> *A loving doe, a graceful deer—*
>> *may her breasts satisfy you always,*
>> *may you ever be captivated by her love.*
> *Why be captivated, my son, by an adulteress?*
>> *Why embrace the bosom of another man's wife?*
> *(Proverbs 5:18-20)*

143

God wants us to enjoy sex, but He wants us to experience it in a marriage relationship. We see that God values the sexual relationship, but within a proper context.

I realize that many of you may have already experimented with your sexuality in ways you wish you hadn't. So many have failed, including leaders we admire, that we think, *Hey, everyone is doing it, and they turned out okay.* I am one of those rare men who actually made it to his wedding day a virgin. I don't say this to brag or pat myself on the back, but I want you to know that what I am going to share was very helpful in my pursuit of purity and continues to be so today. The following principles will help you maintain your purity.

Make a Decision to Wait Until Marriage to Have Sexual Relationships

In the book of Daniel, we are told that Daniel "resolved not to defile himself" (Daniel 1:8) when it came to eating some food that was not good for him to eat, so he made a decision not to eat it. In the same way, we need to make a decision that waiting to have sex is important to us.

When you are on a date or in a relationship, knowing that sex is not an activity you want to participate in at this stage in your life will probably help with 80 percent of the battle. Making a decision helps define your actions, but putting it into practice is another matter.

Watch Your Environment

144 In the seventh chapter of Proverbs, Solomon describes a person he watched being ensnared by an adulteress woman. The victim first allowed himself to be tempted by even being near her. Then he had to deal with the environment she had set up: her spouse was away and she had sprinkled her bed with perfumes and spices.

You won't have others looking out for you, so you have to be careful of your environment. My wife was still in college during our engagement. She had an apartment to herself, so we had to set some boundaries regarding how we spent time together. (If you think waiting for marriage is hard when you are dating, imagine the pressure when you are engaged!) As I left her place one night, a friend of hers was shocked that I was going home rather than just "sleeping over." Her friend assumed we were already sexually active and therefore was amazed when she learned of the boundaries we had set.

Alcohol also creates a dangerous environment for maintaining purity. Judgment can be impaired with only a couple drinks, and even if you choose not to drink, others who do can undergo some changes. Guys can become more aggressive and girls more seductive when under the influence of alcohol, so be careful and control your environment.

Realize That You Are Weak

Even King David, a man after God's heart, committed adultery and caused much pain and anguish in his life (and that of his family too). If King David could become weak enough to act unwisely, so can you. In fact, of all the things that helped me wait until marriage to have sex, realizing my own weakness probably helped me the most. I realized that just because I was a minister and had made the decision to wait didn't mean that if tempted I would be able to resist. So I was very careful and never believed that I was invincible. (Isn't there a proverb that says pride comes before a fall?) In your weakness, rely on God's strength because He will give you what you need to make it through (see Philippians 4:13).

Look for a Way Out

In his letter to the Corinthians, Paul states that any temptation we are presented with is common to human experience and that when we are tempted, God will provide a way of escape (see 1 Corinthians 10:13). So we need to look for a way of escape when we are being tempted, because God said He would provide it.

A guy once told me that because everyone in his family had strong sex drives, he couldn't help but have sex. I laughed and said, "Yeah, you and just about every family I know." It is good to know that the temptations we face have been experienced by others; we are not alone and can find help in talking to others about how they have faced temptations. But God promises not to allow us to face a temptation we cannot resist, so we can't cop out and say the situation was just too overwhelming. God promises an escape route, and we need to find it.

It may be a telephone ring, a simple shove, a needed walk outside (or step out of a car), but God will provide a way out. I was used by God as a way out for others: I called it "lust-busting." Armed with my trusty high-powered halogen flashlight, I would take small groups of students through the parking lot late at night looking for wayward couples spending too much time in their cars. When the moment was right, we all turned on our flashlights. Talk about a mood breaker. Trust me, I did this for fun and not out of a sense of being the "sex police," but looking back, God might have been using my mischief for good.

146

BUT WHAT IF I'VE ALREADY GONE TOO FAR?

Earlier I talked about getting wisdom the "easy way" (through observation and obedience) or the "hard way" (from your own mistakes). Use what you have experienced to gain conviction about your desire for purity. And always remember, God will forgive you for offending Him if you will confess your sins (see 1 John 1:9). Some see this as a free pass to do whatever they wish, but that is not right. Paul sarcastically asked the Romans if we should go on sinning just so we can experience the love of God through forgiveness, and the answer is, "Obviously not" (see Romans 6:1-2). But it is important to seek His forgiveness sincerely and remember that you truly are forgiven by Him and can move on with your life.

Sexual sin has a deep impact on our lives in ways that are difficult to realize. I have met so many guys and girls who have "gone too far" and considered themselves "damaged goods." They wonder how anyone, including God, could ever love them, and the shame they carry is unbearable. The result of this can lead to a downward spiral of self-destruction. Girls believe no decent guy will ever want them, so they allow guys to continue to use them. Other girls deny that what they did impacts them, so they shut down very real emotions, leading to bitterness. Guys can feel shame too, and they may react similarly. They continue to wreck their lives, feeling they now have nothing more to lose. Don't be like these students. Ask for forgiveness, and find a mature Christian of the same sex who you can trust with your story. He or she can help guide you through your pain. (Read chapter 12 for more help on this.)

COULD CELIBACY ACTUALLY BE "THE ONE"?

I promised I'd eventually share where I was going with the percentage-of-males-versus-females-in-the-world idea and what it means about "the one." We don't often talk seriously about this, but it is a very real option and call that God may have for your life. In all my life, I've never heard a sermon preached on Matthew 19:12, but in it, Jesus actually suggests that singleness (eunuchs or renouncers of marriage) can be a calling. Why? "For the sake of the kingdom of heaven" (NASB). Is this perhaps because when we all push our way toward finding "the one," we end up causing more bitterness, jealousy, conniving, and ultimately divorce than not? I honestly don't know, but it's an interesting thought.

Paul, who may very well have been single his whole life, also exclaimed that singleness has its place. He actually encouraged the Corinthians to remain unmarried if at all possible. Being single temporarily or for life provides very unique opportunities to be used by God, and I believe every Christian should consider this possibility. Paul states that the main reason to stay single is that marriage is a whole lot of work: "Those who marry will face many troubles in this life, and I want to spare you this" (1 Corinthians 7:28).

Although I am married now, I took time to seriously consider if remaining single was God's plan for me. Marriage does change our ability to focus solely on matters of serving God. Our concerns increase once we are married (or in a committed relationship, for that matter) (see 1 Corinthians 7:32-35). When I began my life after college, I had an apartment with four folding chairs and a card table, a television propped up by stacks of books, and a futon (which served as a couch and my bed). When I applied for renters insurance, the agent took some Polaroids of the apartment and said, "I'm not sure we can help you; there isn't really anything to insure." But when I got married, a new part of me opened up: the provider. Suddenly I was concerned about things like refrigerators and designer bedspreads, and I even subscribed to Martha Stewart's magazine.

148

I've never gone overboard materialistically, but I am concerned about how I provide for my wife and children (possibly the "finding significance" motivator emerging). I get invited to travel all over the world to participate in great ministry, but I cannot abandon my responsibilities as a husband and father to accept all of the great offers, even if I have space on my calendar. That said, I am glad I am married and am confident it was God's will for my life.

Those who are single should try not to worry about finding "the one" and just take advantage of their singleness. Rather than wallow in self-pity, the wise realize that the freedom offered during singlehood brings opportunities to grow and to serve God.

IT'S A WRAP

Relationships with the opposite sex can really steer you off course during college if you do not align yourself with God's perspective on them. Taking time out from the dating scene and really growing in your walk with God will offer more long-term stability to future relationships. Learn to value what God values regarding marriage and sexuality. Observe the nature of relationships others are engaged in to learn the causes and effects that can help your hookup be free of hang-ups.

THINK ABOUT IT

1. What are your criteria when choosing someone to date? Explain.

2. How do you think dating affects you and your relationships with God and others?

3. How does God want to use dating in your life? How has He used it in the past?

4. What did you learn from this chapter that could apply to your life?

CHAPTER 12

FINDING YODA:
THE VALUE OF A MENTOR

As you are finding your footing in college life, the last subject on your mind may be the idea of listening to someone else's advice. In fact, you're probably still relishing the opposite: *I'm free! It's about time my life is completely up to me. I don't need any more advice.*

Yet here you are, having made it to the end of this book, obviously considering at least some of the guidance offered. And that is the difference, really, between the kind of guidance I'm recommending for you and the kind that's unwanted. You made a choice to read and think about what I had to say. After all, you could've put the book down and never looked at it again. Your willingness to consider my thoughts and experiences is a world away from having others force their uninvited viewpoints on you, right?

So wouldn't it be great to have a source of wisdom at your fingertips on your journey toward wisdom? Someone a little bit further along on the journey than you? Someone to freely offer ideas, thoughts, and decisions? Someone objective? Someone who doesn't judge you? Someone who roots for you and shares your joys and sufferings? Someone who will tell you the truth about yourself? Someone like . . . Yoda?

THE VALUE OF A YODA

I hope you're saying yes right now, because "he who walks with the wise grows wise, but a companion of fools suffers harm"

(Proverbs 13:20). I'm talking about finding a trusted spiritual mentor. No discussion of the development of godly wisdom is complete without acknowledging the importance of finding a true mentor in our lives. And even though the relationship between Luke Skywalker and Yoda is fictional, their interaction in *The Empire Strikes Back* gives us a stimulating picture of how mentoring might work. There are moments when Luke reacts in frustration and anger to Yoda's words and direction. There are moments when Luke's face lights up with discovery and accomplishment. And ultimately, through the good, the bad, and the ugly (no, I'm not talking about that little green guy), Luke comes away from his training not only with increased wisdom and maturity but also with a life enriched by the affection cultivated between him and his mentor.

152

In contrast to his son, Luke, Anakin scorns the guidance of Yoda and his other "Empire" mentors. He pursues the emotional hotbed of romantic love and increasingly makes decisions based on how he feels rather than what is right or best for others. Further, he chooses mentorship by the Emperor, an evil man seeking only self-gain. The result? Anakin's great powers are used for great harm. Finally, when Anakin-turned-Vader realizes that the Emperor will stop at nothing (not even at killing Luke!), Vader realizes the error of his ways and kills the Emperor in order to save Luke's life. It's a gripping and entertaining example of how important the values of our mentors are.

PAUL: CONSUMMATE CHRISTIAN MENTOR

Now, what do we look for in a mentor so that we choose wisely? Obviously, this book suggests we choose someone who is a godly person, someone who knows and lives God's values, and someone who isn't self-righteous or judgmental. There are examples throughout the Bible of mentoring relationships; in fact, among the multitude of roles Jesus Himself exemplified, mentoring was a primary one. (Check out a few of the Gospel stories in which the disciples basically say, "Huh?" to guidance from their leader; note also how Jesus never demeans or speaks down to them.) And then there is Paul, mentor extraordinaire. He sowed seeds of wisdom into many early believers, including Timothy, to the point that they too became effective leaders and ministers of the gospel.

How did he do it? Well, Paul himself had gained wisdom from knowing Christ, coupled with trial-and-error experiences. First, he modeled how to communicate effectively with people, showing his mastery of *justice*. When discussing deep moral and heretical issues occurring in the Corinthian church, instead of being a punishing authoritarian (as he was before his conversion), he instead chose to urge "by the meekness and gentleness of Christ" (2 Corinthians 10:1). He saw the wisdom of being "'timid' when face to face with you, but 'bold' when away!" (2 Corinthians 10:1). He knew the value of listening; otherwise his pastoral letters to Timothy couldn't have been so personal and gentle in encouraging Timothy about his fears.

Second, based on the supreme example of Christ, Paul did not view someone younger or with less experience as inferior. He strove to *value* them as God does. He told Timothy not to look down on his youth but to look to God for his confidence and worth.

Third, Paul also understood from the life of Jesus that we learn well from example and through acting to follow that example (*cause and effect*). Fourth, he recognized that valuing right relationships with God and others is paramount. Before Paul began his ministry as a Christian, he spent years in the mountains of Arabia to get his relationship right with God (see Galatians 1:17-18). He knew from experience the *value* of considering "everything a loss compared to the surpassing greatness of knowing Christ" (Philippians 3:8).

Fifth, he wasn't afraid to let Timothy fail and let God help him grow (*speed bumps*). So even though Timothy was younger and less experienced than Paul, Paul still partnered with him as friend and counselor. Paul trusted God to develop Timothy's wisdom. As an example, Paul gave Timothy the responsibility of checking up on church growth in Thessalonica and other churches (see 1 Thessalonians 3:2). This showed enormous trust, as Paul had spent years of pain, sweat, and suffering to plant and grow these churches. He wouldn't have given Timothy that responsibility if he hadn't believed in him and also trusted God. Now, don't get me wrong: I'm sure there were some hiccups along the way. But the Bible record throughout the Epistles suggests a relationship of trust built on an understanding of each other's strengths and spiritual gifts as well as an openness about their shortcomings.

154

Finally, though we may be mentored in various areas of our lives over the course of our lifetimes, at some point we become mentors too, feeding others what we have learned. Paul understood the *cause-and-effect* principles of mentoring when he wrote to Timothy, "And the things you have heard me say in the presence of many witnesses entrust to reliable men who will also be qualified to teach others" (2 Timothy 2:2). There will be a time when you have wisdom to offer others.

WISE JUMPING-OFF POINTS

I'm sure you now understand that in order to develop wisdom, you must include wise people in your life. Proverbs 12:15 says, "The way of a fool seems right to him, but a wise man listens to advice." Without wise people — mentors — to model your life after, you lack a real-life example, the dynamic presentation of wisdom applied. And your friends, even the best ones, can't always speak wisdom into your life, partly because they're too close to you to see objectively or because they might be afraid to risk the friendship by making unwelcome observations about you.

Now, I don't mean to imply that mentors should tell you what to do. Indeed, if they are good ones, they probably won't tell you what to do but will help guide and support you along your journey. Wise mentors often see you as the best initiator, so before you ask for their input, they likely won't be giving it. In response to the growth you seek, they'll help you explore your options and offer their experience — wise jumping-off points for you to make your own decisions.

So you may be thinking, *Okay, but how exactly does mentoring work? And how do I find a mentor?*

155

DEFINING AND FINDING A MENTOR

Mentoring is a relationship between you and someone more spiritually mature than you in at least one area of your life. There will always be those ahead of you spiritually as well as those behind. Mentors are defined by spiritual maturity and not chronological maturity, though typically someone with more experience than you will have lived longer than you have. For example, you might know someone who has managed the ins and outs of finding a job in his chosen field after college and you'd like to know what he went through to get there. Perhaps someone you know and have admired is now married after setting a godly example in the way he courted his wife. Or you might be dating and need accountability in the area of sexual purity. Perhaps you'd like to explore a spiritual gift you believe God is giving you by talking it over with someone who has had a similar experience. Finally, maybe you have a gossip problem or a fear of praying out loud. Wherever God shows you that you need to grow, a mentor can help facilitate that growth.

A friend of mine, Laura, joined the women's ministry team of her church. Laura did not join with the intent of being mentored; she joined to serve in whatever capacity was needed. But as Laura got to know and respect a woman in the church, she happened to confide to that woman that she had trouble praying one-on-one with another person. The intimacy of just two people intimidated her. At the end of that particular discussion, the person surprised her by saying, "Well, there's no way to learn but by having courage and getting to it, so please, would you close us in prayer?" Gulp! That mature woman, in a gentle but effective way, called Laura to be a better follower of Christ. Laura came away from that experience enriched in two ways: (1) vowing to push beyond her fear and discomfort until the day when praying aloud with another would come easily to her, and (2) experiencing firsthand the reward of a mentoring relationship. We can learn from anybody, not just those we have agreed to be mentored by.

However, mentoring works best when you and your mentor set clear parameters for your relationship. What are your expectations of a mentor? Ask God to reveal exactly what it is you seek from a mentor, and investigate your hidden motives with His help. Your mentor will not be a parent and won't necessarily tell you what to do in a difficult situation. Primarily, in an ideal mentoring relationship, you and your mentor will do the following:

- Sign a covenant of confidentiality and write a contract detailing the areas of your life you would like to work on (where you want better alignment).
- Define expectations. You will need someone "safe" who will allow you to honestly express yourself and who will value relationship with you over lecturing you on your wrongdoing or over arguing religious doctrine.
- Identify specific ways you might achieve your goals, for example, by reading a Christian book together, doing a Bible study, or performing acts of service together.
- Develop an honest description of your personality style and how to best hold you accountable. For example, do you need gentle prodding or brutal honesty?
- Establish a regular meeting schedule. Every two weeks or once a month is ideal.
- Set ways to measure your progress and agree to a limited mentoring time frame (such as six months) so that you can **157** reevaluate when the time is up.

Cultivating a humble heart means getting the most out of a mentoring relationship. "When pride comes, then comes disgrace, but with humility comes wisdom" (Proverbs 11:2). Being strong in your convictions sometimes means having the courage to listen to others when they're pointing out an area of your life that makes you squirm. Mentoring does include healthy boundaries, but if you shut down every time you hear something uncomfortable about yourself, you might not be ready for a mentoring relationship. Before you get involved, ask the Holy Spirit to help you know yourself: your weaknesses, your strengths, and where you need to grow.

Finding a mentor is easier than you might think. Some of my mentors have been professors, pastors at any level, or other church laypersons who I began to admire. For all of them, the key aspect I was attracted to was their clear love for God and others, and their willingness to listen and not just give advice. God created us to encourage one another in our Christian lives, for as Paul the great mentor wrote, "Praise be to the God and Father of our Lord Jesus Christ, the Father of compassion and the God of all comfort, who comforts us in all our troubles, so that we can comfort those in any trouble with the comfort we ourselves have received from God" (2 Corinthians 1:3-4). When we comfort people, we love them and we listen.

To find a mentor, all you have to do is pay attention. When you see and admire someone's relationship with God (including his or her words and actions), that person might make a good mentor. But remember that accurately evaluating character is critical to finding a good mentor. Don't be impatient with yourself; character evaluation is part of the wisdom process. But please use the guidelines I presented in chapter 9 about looking for words, actions, reactions, and directions. Also, pray a lot and be "as shrewd as snakes and as innocent as doves" (Matthew 10:16) just as Jesus advised His disciples as He sent them into the world.

Most of all, don't be shy. When you think you've spotted a potential mentor, pray about it and, with God's green light, tell him or her that you're interested in creating a mentoring relationship. If a face-to-face conversation is difficult, use e-mail. God will use your mentoring relationship to foster some exciting wisdom growth in your life. I promise, if you're a willing student, you won't wait long to see that fruit in your life!

PARENTAL MENTORS: AN OXYMORON?

It might be hard to swallow right now, but even our parents can offer us a certain kind of mentoring. I know, I know—you've just gotten out from under their sometimes stuffy wings. So take a step back if you need to. That's okay. But when you've had time to gain some objectivity about them as individuals and not just as the parental unit, take a look at their lives and check out what they have to offer. It might surprise you. Or if you've always appreciated them for their input, great! Either way, it would be a mistake to reject the wisdom they've gained in life just because they cooed over your baby pictures with your first girlfriend or showed pictures of your tomboy days to your first boyfriend.

My parents actually wanted me to go to college farther away from home than I did—not because they didn't want me around but because they wanted me to be able to stand on the foundation they had given me. In the middle of my freshman year at Biola, I felt God leading me away from one major to another. I listened to an anthropologist whose work fascinated me, and I could see myself studying the ways people think, act, and relate. It seemed to be a perfect fit for my long-term goals, but for some reason, I just didn't feel right about it. For a week, I stayed up late at night, thinking and praying. I was exhausted, but I still wasn't sure what to do. At about one o'clock in the morning, I called my dad and told him I needed to talk to him about something important. He got out of bed and drove forty minutes to see me, and we talked about my future for a couple of hours. I'm not sure what meant more to me that night: the wise direction that he provided or the fact that he was glad to get out of bed in the middle of the night to come and talk to me. Both were instrumental in not only helping me make my decision but also in shaping my life as a whole.

My dad played the mentor simply by being there for me through a tough decision. He also played the mentor by offering me options and guidance and helping me clarify my thoughts. I ended up changing my major to anthropology, and that eventually led to the career path I am presently on (like most college graduates, I do not work in the area of my major, but my major led me to the ministry I am now in). As we mature, our parents can become less parental and more like the mentors we need in life.

GIVING GOD LATITUDE

I hope by now you're convinced that if you want to know God better and expedite your character development under God's wise hand, you should seek out a mentoring relationship. By doing so, you'll give God the amazing latitude to form wisdom in you. Make a commitment to ask hard questions and then be willing to wrestle with the answers. Be ready to struggle through some difficult times to see what God might be trying to do. But don't worry if you don't find answers right away or if life seems to get more complex every day. Trust God. He will mold into you the wisdom of Jesus hour by hour, day by day. Wisdom takes time! It takes a lifetime.

THINK ABOUT IT

1. What thoughts do you have about getting a mentor? What criteria are particularly important to you when choosing one?

2. Is there anyone in your life who you think could mentor you? What would you want to talk about with him or her?

3. How do you think having a mentor could affect you and your relationships with God and others?

161

4. What did you learn from this chapter that could apply to your life?

LIFE IN ALL ITS FULLNESS IS THE DESTINATION

Anytime you go through a major transition in life, it is very easy to get out of alignment with God. Entering into college life is definitely a time of major change, but it does not give you a free pass to walk away from God.

While my desire has been to help you think about some situations you'll encounter before they become issues, there are so many more issues you could potentially face that I have not addressed here. Using the points of reference (cause and effect, justice, and values) and speed bumps, you can develop wisdom every day no matter what situation you might face.

Wisdom comes from the ability to make observations about life: the more intentional your observations, the faster you reach maturity. Two observational habits have helped me in my life, which I will leave you with.

1. PROJECTION

The art of projection involves imagining yourself in a position before you are actually there. In section 2, I discussed several topics—for example, friendships, dating relationships, use of time—that may present new issues central to your life. Think about these matters before they become problems, and project what you would do and how you would handle yourself if they were to happen.

Projection can help you act wisely before you are under the pressure of having to act. Use the three points of reference to help "walk you through" a situation before you actually experience it. For instance, knowing that the opportunity for alcohol abuse or for sexual activity outside of marriage could increase in the college setting, consider what you might do before there is a problem. Maybe you have a policy not to attend social functions where alcohol is present. Or perhaps you decide that you will never be alone in your dorm room with a member of the opposite sex.

2. REFLECTION

Take time to review your day and learn from it. A mistake can be a very good thing if you learn from it, and often successes can be repeated if you understand what led to that result. It's also valuable to reflect on the life experiences of others. Examine the past using the three points of reference with the idea that God is trying to work in your life (mystery/speed bumps). I try to make reflection a nightly habit so that I learn the most from each day. Remember to consider the types of questions you might be using during your reflection time. Are they heavenly minded or worldly minded?

164

Most of all, enjoy your years in college—they are like no other time in your life. As Solomon wrote toward the end of Ecclesiastes, "Let your heart give you joy in the days of your youth. Follow the ways of your heart and whatever your eyes see, but know that for all these things God will bring you to judgment. . . . Remember your Creator in the days of your youth" (Ecclesiastes 11:9; 12:1). In doing so, you will start off your wisdom journey well and experience true fullness of life.

A SUGGESTED READING LIST
FOR FURTHERING YOUR WISDOM JOURNEY

Dietrich Bonhoeffer, *The Cost of Discipleship* (Touchstone, 1995) — a compelling and challenging look at what it means to be a true disciple of Christ.

Scott R. Burson and Jerry L. Walls, *C. S. Lewis and Francis Schaeffer: Lessons for a New Century from the Most Influential Apologists of Our Time* (InterVarsity, 1998) — compares and contrasts each author's contribution in light of new postmodern thinking.

John Eldredge, *The Journey of Desire: Searching for the Life We Only Dreamed Of* (Nelson, 2000) — an invitation to rediscover God-given desire and to search again for the life you once dreamed of.

John Eldredge, *Wild at Heart: Discovering the Secret of a Man's Soul* (Nelson, 2001) — a look into what men are searching for as a way to find male identity.

Garry Friesen and J. Robin Maxon, *Decision Making and the Will of God: A Biblical Alternative to the Traditional View* (Multnomah, 1999) — a way of looking at God's will for your life in a freeing and practical way.

C. S. Lewis, *A Grief Observed* (HarperSanFrancisco, 2001)—an authentic look into C. S. Lewis's loss of his wife. He explores how to relate honestly to God when emotions are flaring. It is like reading his diaries after his wife died, when he began to question God's goodness.

C. S. Lewis, *Mere Christianity* (HarperSanFrancisco, 2001)—great insights into the essentials of Christianity.

C. S. Lewis, *The Problem of Pain* (HarperSanFrancisco, 2001)—a rational look at why God allows suffering. Interesting to read accompanied by *A Grief Observed*.

C. S. Lewis, *The Screwtape Letters* (HarperSanFrancisco, 2001)—great insights into human motivations creatively expressed as a dialogue between two demons.

Eric and Leslie Ludy, *When God Writes Your Love Story: The Ultimate Approach to Guy/Girl Relationships* (Multnomah, 2004)—an honest, open, and funny read about the authors' journey to include God in their romantic pursuits.

Leslie Ludy, *Authentic Beauty: The Shaping of a Set-Apart Young Woman* (Multnomah, 2003)—a look into what women are searching for as a way to find female identity.

Gordon MacDonald, *Ordering Your Private World* (Nelson, 2003)—a practical look at why we need to carve out time for God in our lives.

Rabi R. Maharaj, *Death of a Guru* (Harvest House, 2003)—an autobiography of a young Hindu's search for truth.

J. P. Moreland, *Love Your God with All Your Mind: The Role of Reason in the Life of the Soul* (NavPress, 1997)—seeing the value of using our head when we relate to God and others.

Lesslie Newbigin, *The Gospel in a Pluralist Society* (Eerdmans, 1989)—covers a missionary's heart to understand the gospel despite the pluralist culture surrounding him.

J. I. Packer, *Knowing God* (InterVarsity, 1993)—a classic overview of God's character.

Hugh Ross, *A Matter of Days: Resolving a Creation Controversy* (NavPress, 2004)—a balanced argument for God's existence through creation using science.

Lee Strobel, *The Case for Christ: A Journalist's Personal Investigation of the Evidence for Jesus* (Zondervan, 1998)—a well-written and entertaining story of Strobel's journey to understand if we can trust the Bible and the stories about Jesus.

167

Lauren F. Winner, *Girl Meets God: On a Path to a Spiritual Life* (Shaw, 2004)—an autobiography of her spiritual journey.

Philip Yancey, *Disappointment with God: Three Questions No One Asks Aloud* (Zondervan, 1997)—a journey through God's mystery and how it can frustrate us when we don't understand what God values.

Philip Yancey, *The Jesus I Never Knew* (Zondervan, 2002)—the author's journey to understand what we can learn from how Jesus lived.

Philip Yancey, *What's So Amazing About Grace?* (Zondervan, 2002) — a provocative look at why grace is one of the most needed, yet most absent, attributes of the church.

NOTES

CHAPTER 1

1. Malcolm Gladwell, *The Tipping Point: How Little Things Can Make a Big Difference* (Boston: Little, Brown, 2002).

CHAPTER 2

1. J. I. Packer, *Knowing God* (Downers Grove, Ill.: InterVarsity, 1973).

CHAPTER 5

1. George Barna, *The Frog in the Kettle* (Ventura, Calif.: Regal, 1990).
2. John Bunyan, *The Pilgrim's Progress* (Oxford University, 1998).

CHAPTER 6

1. Richard A. Swenson, *More Than Meets the Eye: Fascinating Glimpses of God's Power and Design* (Colorado Springs, Colo.: NavPress, 2000).
2. William Lane Craig, *Hard Questions, Real Answers* (Wheaton, Ill.: Crossway, 2003).
3. Philip Yancey, *Disappointment with God* (Grand Rapids, Mich.: Zondervan, 1997).
4. Francis I. Anderson, *Job* (TOTC) (Downers Grove, Ill.: InterVarsity, 1976).
5. St. John of the Cross, transcribed by E. Allison Peers (New York: Bantam Dell Doubleday, 1990).

CHAPTER 7

1. C. S. Lewis, *A Grief Observed* (San Francisco: HarperSanFrancisco, 2001).

2. Philip Yancey, as quoted in "An Unnatural Act," by Margaret Gramatky Alter, *Christianity Today*, April 8, 1991, p. 37.

3. Frederick Buechner, *Wishful Thinking: A Theological ABC* (San Francisco: HarperSanFrancisco, 1993), p. 2.

4. Matthew Josephson, *Edison: A Biography* (New York: John Wiley and Sons, 1992).

5. Thomas Watson, Sr., as quoted in *Whoever Makes the Most Mistakes Wins: The Paradox of Innovation*, by Richard Farson and Ralph Keyes (New York: Free Press/Simon and Schuster, 2002).

CHAPTER 8

1. C. S. Lewis, *A Grief Observed* (San Francisco: HarperSanFrancisco, 2001).

CHAPTER 9

1. www.quoteworld.org.

2. *The Essays (1625)*, Francis Bacon, (Penguin Books, 1986).

3. www.worldofquotes.com.

4. C. S. Lewis, *The Four Loves* (Nashville: W Publishing, 1994), p. 65.

CHAPTER 11

1. Larry Crabb, *Understanding People: Why We Long for Relationship* (Grand Rapids, Mich: Zondervan, 1987).

2. Crabb.

ABOUT THE AUTHOR

For more than a decade, Mark Matlock has ministered full-time to youth pastors and students using his remarkable teaching style to present biblical truths in ways that motivate change in believers' lives. He is president and founder of WisdomWorks Ministries, creator of planetwisdom.com, coauthor with Audio Adrenaline of *Dirty Faith: Becoming the Hands and Feet of Jesus,* and a columnist for *Campus Life* magazine. Mark has spoken face-to-face with thousands of students nationally and internationally at his PlanetWisdom events. He also hosts a nationally syndicated radio show called *WisdomWorks.* He resides in Irving, Texas, with his wife, Jade, and their two children, Dax and Skye Dawn.

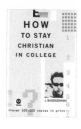